Mighty Minutes

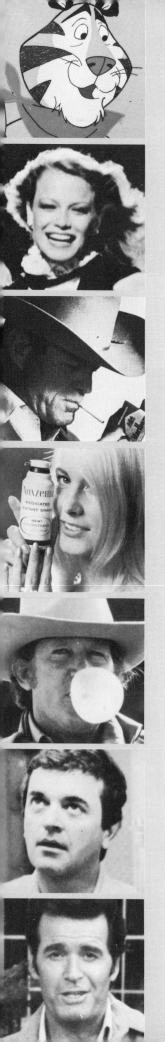

Mighty

An Illustrated History of

By Jim Hall

Minutes

Television's Best Commercials

HARMONY BOOKS · NEW YORK

Dedicated to Thomas Graham, Jr.

Published by Harmony Books, a division of Crown Publishers, Inc.,
One Park Avenue, New York, New York 10016 and simultaneously in
Canada by General Publishing Company Limited.

HARMONY and colophon are trademarks of Crown Publishers, Inc.

Manufactured in the United States of America

Library of Congress Cataloging in Publication Data

Hall, Jim, 1954-
    Mighty minutes.

    1. Television advertising—United States—History.
I. Title.
HF6146.T42H33 1984   649.14′3′0973   83-26441
ISBN 0-517-55318-X (pbk.)

Book designed by Cynthia Eyring

10 9 8 7 6 5 4 3 2 1

First Edition

Contents

Acknowledgments

We wish to thank the following people and organizations. Credits are listed picture by picture for each corresponding page (left to right, top to bottom).

ILLUSTRATIONS

Title page Tony®the Tiger is a registered trademark of Kellogg Company/©Revlon, Inc., Charlie Commercials Courtesy of Revlon, Inc./"Reprinted by permission of Philip Morris, Incorporated"/©Noxell Corporation 1966/W.M. Wrigley, Jr. Co./©1978 The Gillette Company/Copyright ©1980 Polaroid Corporation

12 Tony®the Tiger is a trademark of Kellogg Company

13 The Jolly Green Giant figure is a registered trademark of The Green Giant Company. ©The Green Giant Company 1976/The Procter & Gamble Company

14 The Quaker Oats Company/The Quaker Oats Company

15 Planters and Mr. Peanut are registered trademarks of Nabisco Brands, Inc.

16–17 By permission of Texaco Inc./Colgate-Palmolive Co.

18 Lorillard, Div. of Loews' Theatres, Inc./"Courtesy of Carnation Company"

18–19 ©1983 Miles Laboratories, Inc. Consumer Healthcare Division

19 *Unconfirmed*/Ford Motor Company

20 ©The Gillette Company. Used with the permission of The Gillette Company. All rights reserved/Courtesy Anheuser-Busch, Inc.

21 *Unconfirmed*

22 Wally, the Western Airlines' bird, is a registered service mark of Western Airlines, Inc., 6060 Avion Drive, Los Angeles, California 90045

23 Pabst Brewing Company

24 G. Heileman Brewing Company, Inc./THE CAMPBELL KIDS, trademarks of Campbell Soup Company, have been reproduced with its express permission

25 *Tony®the Tiger* is a trademark of Kellogg Company

26 *Snap!®*, *Crackle!®*, *Pop!®* are trademarks of Kellogg Company

27 Colgate-Palmolive Co./©The Pillsbury Company 1982/©The Pillsbury Company 1982

28 "Charlie the Tuna" is a registered trademark of Star-Kist Foods, Inc. ©STAR-KIST FOODS, INC. 1976

28–29 "Morris the Cat" is a registered trademark of Star-Kist Foods, Inc.

29 ®©1968, Frito-Lay, Inc.

30 Copyright: Qantas Airways

31 ©1955 S.C. Johnson & Son, Inc.

32 The Hartford Insurance Group/The Dreyfus Corporation

33 Merrill Lynch

34 The Procter & Gamble Company

35 The Quaker Oats Company

36 Photo Courtesy The Maytag Company

37 The Procter & Gamble Company

38 The Procter & Gamble Company

39 Union Underwear Company, Inc.

40 Union Underwear Company, Inc.

41 Xerox Corporation

42 ©Revlon, Inc., Charlie Commercials Courtesy of Revlon, Inc.

43 ©Clairol, Inc./JELL-O is a registered trademark of General Foods Corporation, White Plains, New York. Advertisements courtesy of General Foods Corporation

44 *Unconfirmed*

45 Pet Incorporated/*Unconfirmed*

46 JELL-O is a registered trademark of General Foods Corporation, White Plains, New York. Advertisements courtesy of General Foods Corporation/Chevrolet Motor Division, General Motors Corporation

47 Westinghouse Electric Corporation

48 "Courtesy of General Mills"

49 Bardahl Mfg. Corp., 1400 N.W. 52nd Street, Seattle, Washington 98107/Bardahl Mfg. Corp., 1400 N.W. 52nd Street, Seattle, Washington 98107

50 Reproduced with permission of the Goodyear Tire & Rubber Company—All Rights Reserved/Reproduced with permission of the Goodyear Tire & Rubber Company —All Rights Reserved/Reproduced with permission of the Goodyear Tire & Rubber Company—All Rights Reserved

51 ©Clairol, Inc.

52 Colgate-Palmolive Co.

53 ©Clairol, Inc.

55 "Reprinted by permission of Philip Morris Incorporated."

56 Used with the permission of the Copyright Owner, Charles of the Ritz Group Ltd. ©1978

58 ©Revlon, Inc., Charlie Commercials Courtesy of Revlon, Inc.

59 ©Revlon, Inc., Charlie Commercials Courtesy of Revlon, Inc.

60 "Reprinted by permission of Philip Morris, Incorporated"

61 ©Miller Brewing Company/Malt-O-Meal Company, Minneapolis, Minnesota

62 The American Tobacco Company, A Division of American Brands, Inc./"Courtesy of General Mills"

63 Courtesy of Timex Corporation

64–65 Copyright by Allstate Insurance Company, Northbrook, Illinois

66 "Reprinted by permission of Philip Morris, Incorporated"

66–67 Richardson-Vicks, Inc., Wilton, CT
67 Richardson-Vicks, Inc., Wilton, CT
68 Kentucky Fried Chicken/Kentucky Fried Chicken
69 Minute Maid is a registered trademark of the Coca-Cola Company/Minute Maid is a registered trademark of the Coca-Cola Company
70 "Courtesy of General Mills"
71 Chrysler Corporation Photo
72 Chrysler Corporation Photo
73 Shell Oil Company
75 Photo courtesy of British Airways
76 The Quaker Oats Company
77 Ford Motor Company
78 Malt-O-Meal Company, Minneapolis, Minnesota
80 ©Miller Brewing Company 1982
81 ©Miller Brewing Company 1982
82 Courtesy of Hanes Group
83 ©Noxell Corporation 1966/Serta, Inc.
84–85 Boyle-Midway
85 Consolidated Cigar Co.
86 ©Noxell Corporation 1966/Beecham, Inc.
88 Serta, Inc.
89 Ace Hardware Corporation/Serta, Inc.
90 Consolidated Cigar Co.
91 Courtesy of Hanes Group
92 ©The Wella Corporation, Englewood, NJ
93 ©Jovan, Inc.
94–95 ©1980 Par Parfums Ltd.
96 Chanel, Inc.
97 Chanel, Inc.
98 Reprinted with permission by PepsiCo, Inc., Purchase, NY
99 Chanel, Inc.
100 W.M. Wrigley, Jr. Co.
101 Toucan Sam® is a trademark of Kellogg Company/ "Courtesy of General Mills"
102 Mattel, Inc.
103 Ovaltine Products, Inc.
104–105 Copyright © 1959 by The Seven-Up Company
104–105 "Copyright 1958 Kellogg Company." Tony® the Tiger, Coco®, Snap!®, Crackle!®, Pop!®, Sugar Pops Pete®, Smaxie®, and Cornelius are trademarks of Kellogg Company.
106 "Copyright 1983 Kellogg Company"/Toucan Sam®, Snap!®, Crackle!®, Poppy®, Tony® the Tiger, Dig'em®, Tony, Jr.® and Pop!®./"Copyright 1953 Kellogg Company"
107 Standard Milling Division of the Uhlmann Co./ "Copyright 1958 Kellogg Company." Sugar Pops Pete® is a trademark of Kellogg Company
108 Beatrice Confections Division, Beatrice Foods Company, 1600 North Broadway, St. Louis, Mo. 63102
109 Malt-O-Meal Company, Minneapolis, Minnesota/ ©1960 Del Monte Corporation
110 "Courtesy of General Mills"

111 "Courtesy of General Mills"
112 The Quaker Oats Company
113–114 The Quaker Oats Company/The Quaker Oats Company
114 "Courtesy of General Mills"
115 McDonald's Corporation/McDonald's Corporation
116 ©The Burger King Corporation. All Rights reserved
117 ©Toys "Я" Us, Inc. 1981. ©Toys "Я" Us, Inc. 1981
119 W.M. Wrigley, Jr. Co.
120 ©1978 The Gillette Company
121 ©1983 Miles Laboratories, Inc. Consumer Health Care Division/Copyright © 1974 by The Seven-Up Company
122–125 Courtesy Stan Freberg, Freberg Ltd.
127 ©1978 The Gillette Company
128 Federal Express Corp.
129 Federal Express Corp.
130 Federal Express Corp.
132 JELL-O is a registered trademark of General Foods Corporation, White Plains, New York. Advertisements courtesy of General Foods Corporation./JELL-O is a registered trademark of General Foods Corporation, White Plains, New York. Advertisements courtesy of General Foods Corporation.
133 Chevrolet Motor Division, General Motors Corporation
134 Chevrolet Motor Division, General Motors Corporation
135 Courtesy Volkswagen of America
136 Courtesy Volkswagen of America
137 Copyright © 1974 by The Seven-Up Company
138 Kawasaki Motors Corp., U.S.A.
139 "Authorized by Levi Straus & Co."
140 "Authorized by Levi Straus & Co."
140–145 ©1983 Miles Laboratories, Inc. Consumer Health Care Division.
146 Copyright ©1980 Polaroid Corporation
147 General Electric Co/©Oscar Mayer & Co., Inc.
148 Rice-A-Roni is a registered trademark of the Golden Grain Macaroni Co. and is used with the Company's permission.
149 ©Hertz System, Inc. 1983
151 ©Hertz System, Inc. 1983
152 ©Oscar Mayer & Co. Inc./©Oscar Mayer & Co. Inc.
154 Courtesy of the Archives: The Coca-Cola Company/Courtesy of the Archives: The Coca-Cola Company
155 California & Hawaii Sugar Co.
156 General Electric Co.
157–158 ©Copyright Eastern Kodak Company 1969
160 Copyright ©1969 Polaroid Corporation/Copyright ©1980 Polaroid Corporation
162 Hallmark Cards, Inc.
163–164 Reprinted with permission by PepsiCo, Inc., Purchase, NY

LYRICS

Credits for lyrics are listed by corresponding page (left to right, top to bottom).

Mighty Minutes

Introduction

The average American watches television an incredible six hours a day. A great deal of what is seen are commercials. For the most part, these video ads inundate viewers and are often shrieking irritants. Yet there exists a well-crafted, witty minority whose jingles we sing, whose jokes we repeat, and whose special effects dazzle us. Certainly, more care and craftsmanship are lavished on each second of the best of television's commercials than on any other film form, including television programming and theatrical motion pictures. Thematically, the best commercials also convey something pithy but intricately observed about the American life-style.

Fundamentally, and contrary to the benign popular myth, television is not an artistic medium, or one whose purpose is to entertain or to convey information. It is an advertising medium. Commercial television, as its name suggests, owes its existence to its sponsors. It hardly matters to advertisers what type of moronity is aired by the networks, as long as consumers continue to watch. In fact, witless, bland-looking programs make well-made commercials stand out like sparkling gems. If viewers were content to sit before test patterns, then sponsors would find no reason to object. Similarly, if viewers were to abandon the medium en masse, disgusted (an unlikely proposition, so tolerant are we of free entertainment), then the Procter & Gambles and Colgate-Palmolives would soon be sending their representatives to the networks demanding "quality television." But in our democracy, not only the elected officials but the programs flitting across the public airwaves are ensconced by popular mandate.

The best video ads are not produced as entertainment or as art, though surely they are both. Commercials are born of the specific mercantile need to sell products. They communicate news to consumers who, thus informed, buy goods. Inventories move, profits rise, the gross national product expands, and the relentless march of human progress takes another step. Mounted as they are with the precision and earnestness of military operations, it is no wonder that commercial stratagems are referred to by their creators as "campaigns." Commercials wage constant warfare against their competitors on the air and the terminal spectre of viewer apathy.

To wage these campaigns, commercial-makers employ a number of "sub-genres," of which the identifiable-character ads represent commercials' chief contribution to popular art. The ID character, if successful, not only brings to mind the sponsor's product, creating a strong association, but exists as a video folk hero, like Morris the Cat or Charlie the Tuna. Testimonial commercials, either by actors impersonating "real" people endorsing a product, or by celebrities testifying for a sponsor, are the workhorses of commercials. Also common are the demonstration commercials, which show the product in use, either in conventional or exaggerated circumstances. "Dramatic" commercials, which may be humorous as well as touching, are "minute movies" of theatrical quality in script, music, direction, acting, and visual effects. A lesser form of the "dramatic" commercial is the standard "problem-solving" ad in which a crisis is neatly and expeditiously resolved by quick application of the sponsor's product. The most primitive commercial species is the "hard sell" ad, featuring the authoritative spokesman "pitching" his product, often accompanied by graphs and a jumble of statistics.

The process of commercial-making is fairly standardized. In the beginning, we have the advertising agency account executives huddling with their clients in boardrooms, brainstorming different strategies to promote their client's product until one concept emerges triumphant from the fray. Perhaps the agreed-upon commercial will feature a celebrity pitchman, an animated identifiable character, or a jingle. The agency art director and the agency copywriter will then concoct a storyboard. This is a comic-strip version of the completed commercial, and it is used by the agency producer to execute a "test commercial." Usually, three or four of these crude sample ads are produced and shown to sample audiences. Depending upon how well the commercial is remembered by these viewers, it is rated numerically. The ad with the highest score is filmed by a production company, at an average 1983 cost of $90,000 per thirty-second ad, and made into the finished commercial, ready for airing. Just as the Nielson ratings determine which television program will succeed, advertising testing services determine what commercial a sponsor will air. This spares the ad agency personnel the trauma of making that creative decision.

The completed commercial that then becomes a part of the viewers' six-hour daily habit will more often than not capitalize upon their hygienic, financial, sexual, and intellectual insecurities. The commercial will also reinforce the American tribal maxim that to be a good citizen-consumer, the viewer's home must abound with sponsors' products, so lavishly displayed on the television bazaar.

Popular art, or "pop art," may be defined as anarchic art, media created without the systematism and discipline of the traditional "fine arts" (sculpture, music, painting, etc.). Pop art is nonetheless born of creative impulses and is widely, if faddishly, accepted by mass audiences. (There was no pop art before the era of mass communications.) Whichever medium enjoys popularity at any given time in society—movies, radio dramas, TV, video arcade games, and so on—enters the realm of popular culture. Bright, tawdry, ephemeral, these pop arts represent one-half of contemporary society's bread-and-circuses formula. In commercials, which employ the techniques of the filmmaker to sell consumer goods, both the bread and the circus are on display.

Unlike other forms of popular culture—films, for instance—TV commercials have not enjoyed systematic preservation by anyone, save a few private collectors and professional archives. As a result, much of the work produced over the years has been lost. Sponsors, who hardly see themselves as producers of art, popular or otherwise, feel that once a commercial has fulfilled its sales objective, it is a dead property not worth the storage cost. And the advertising agencies, those gypsies of the business world, dance from account to account, and routinely toss out works they have produced for old clients. Thus has the institutionalized myopia of American business succeeded in effacing a piece of history, its own as well as ours. The number and variety of illustrations that are to be found in this volume represent the fruits of an intensive and extensive period of detective work that is all the more extraordinary because so many of the "lost" commercials were produced only a few years ago.

This is, of course, regrettable, since commercials present to us, in microcosmic but vivid form, a social and economic record of America during the television age: the changing roles of men and women in our culture, the storybook fantasies that have beguiled generations of youthful Kid Vid viewers, and the evolution of styles and sensibilities. Certainly these thirty- and sixty-second "time capsules" are nostalgic and entertaining. More important, though, they reflect an idealized but remarkably cogent view of a society whose video-addicted citizens have come to accept commercials as fixtures of their daily lives. For something so ubiquitous, television commercials, which display not-so-rare flashes of creative genius, are truly "the pop art that nobody knows."

Chapter One

The Identifiable Characters

"From Valley of

The pop art of television commercials has had its share of "classics" over the last thirty-five years. The commercials' version of the Oscars, the CLIO Awards (named after the mythological Greek muse of history), are given annually for outstanding video ads. The international film festivals at Cannes and Venice also cite the best commercials each

the
the Jolly…"

year. Yet it is the American televiewer who ultimately determines which ads are the all-time favorites. A commercial featuring an identifiable character as popular as the Jolly Green Giant® will remain on the air for decades. An ill-favored ad may not only have a short life, but might jeopardize the sponsor's product.

Word of mouth, the best of sales tools, indicates a commercial's popularity. A hit is at hand if conversation stops when the commercial appears on the screen, or when phrases like "try it, you'll like it" pop up in casual conversation. Often a commercial is a hit because of its characters. From the advertiser's point of view, these characters are memorable, and viewers become easily attached to them. In fact, products represented by an identifiable character are remembered longer than products sold by a jingle or celebrity endorsement.

The earliest identifiable characters of the mass media were the elephant and donkey symbols of the Republican and Democratic parties. Both were first seen in newspaper cartoons in the late nineteenth century. Like the venerable donkey and elephant, many of advertising's very first ID characters have become institutions. But while these grand old company-identifiable characters have been enshrined as familiar bits of Americana, not all have achieved success in television commercials. Video was never the home for Elsie the Cow, Aunt Jemima, or the Smith Brothers.

The Quaker Man—the Benjamin Franklin look-alike whose gentle smile, ruddy cheeks, and tricornered hat have graced oatmeal boxes since the 1880s—has proved more adaptable. His transition from the print media to TV commercials was, however, limited. No actor could adequately impersonate him. As explained by Elizabeth Harrington, Quaker's current vice-president in charge of advertising: "You can't make a larger-than-life character real and believable. He becomes mundane and pedestrian. People would look at him and feel we've failed to meet their expectations."

The Quaker Man, a Benjamin Franklin look-alike, has graced oatmeal boxes for five generations. (Ad Com, 1984)

Whenever viewers see or hear an identifiable character, they should think of the product that is associated with that character.

An ID character can be portrayed by a familiar character actor, an animated creature, an animal, or an anthropomorphic product. No amount of contrivance, however, will assure the success of an ID character. Its popularity

The Quaker Man as he first appeared in the 1880s, as one of advertising's first, and certainly most enduring, identifiable characters.

A partial solution was found by showing only the portrait of the Quaker Man (familiar now to five generations of Americans) that appears on the label of the cylindrical oatmeal box.

among viewers can only be the result of the appeal of its personality. A memorable ID character cannot be a caricature, but must be an individual with human emotions. The more human an ID character is, the greater will be the number of dramatic situations available for its involvement, and so will the character's popularity continue to captivate viewers for a long period of time. Once an identifiable character's popularity is established, it becomes a lucrative and enduring advertising commodity, one whose "wear-out factor" is postponed. Over the Quaker Man's face a deep voice intoned, "Nothing is better for thee than me," an otherwise presumptuous claim that, by a combination of nostalgia and sincerity, managed to ring true.

Mr. Peanut also found a new advertising career in commercials, becoming television's smallest identifiable character. Peanut came into being in 1916, when the Planters Nut and Chocolate Company of Wilkes-Barre, Pennsylvania, held a contest to come up with a suitable trademark to promote its salted Virginia peanuts. The winning entry was submitted by a fourteen-year-old schoolboy who drew an anthropomorphic peanut, a "dandy" in a top hat. Mr. Peanut, as he was subsequently named, became known internationally. He appeared in his first television commercial in the early fifties, tap-dancing around a bottle of peanut oil.

Debonair Mr. Peanut, complete with top hat, monocle, spats, white gloves, and cane, is the best-dressed identifiable character. (Benton & Bowles, 1960)

But there was little that writers could do with an identifiable character who, by tradition, could not speak. Mr. Peanut was rarely seen on TV until he appeared as an animated doll to commemorate Planters' seventy-fifth anniversary in 1981. This newest Mr. Peanut led a chorus, using his cane for a baton, in an upbeat birthday song. A definitive personality had at last emerged for Peanut: the aristocratic spright, the miniature butler always happy to serve snacks and hors d'oeuvres.

THE FIRST ID CHARACTERS

On the night of June 8, 1948, network television's first year, the curtain went up on the live
premiere program of *The Texaco Star Theater*,
starring Milton Berle. A quartet of service-
station attendants stood before a painted backdrop and sang: "Oh, we're the men from
Texaco/We work from Maine to Mexico/
There's nothing like this Texaco of ours . . ."

   After their opening number on television's
first variety show, the four servicemen in their
forest-green uniforms introduced "Uncle
Milty," a former vaudevillian who became so
popular in the new medium that he earned the
name "Mr. Television." At the end of each
show, the quartet returned to sing good night.

   The servicemen did not, however, sing "You
can trust your car to the man who wears the
star/The big, bright Texaco Star," a jingle not
heard until the early sixties. The quartet established itself as a fixture in the first five years of
television. A sheen of nostalgia surrounds the
servicemen now—they are a part of television's
Golden Age. Recognizing the servicemen's appeal, Texaco's agency, Benton &
Bowles, revived them in 1982 to open and close
the new *Texaco Star Theater*. The jingle they
performed was vintage forties, but the costumes
and the inclusion of a pert blond "service-
woman" updated the image of both the quartet
and the company.

**From 1948 through 1953, the Texaco
quartet became fixtures on television.
(Benton & Bowles, 1948)**

**The Ajax Pixies. Notice that the large
pixie obscures the product's name,
thereby breaking one of commercials'
elementary rules. The Pixies helped
around the kitchen as commercials'
first animated ID characters in gag-
filled ads that began running in 1948.
(Ted Bates, 1948)**

In those primitive days of television, Bill Hertz was in charge of designing storyboards, or visual scripts, for Pixie commercials. Today he is an animator for Jay Ward Productions, the studio that has produced such Kid Vid heroes as Rocky and Bullwinkle and Cap'n Crunch. Hertz's inventive storyboards included such gags as one pixie, admiring his reflection on a pot he had just cleaned, taking a sparkling star of light from the glistening bright metal and pinning it proudly to his shirt like a badge. Such endearing humor did much to condition early audiences to be receptive to sponsors' messages.

Another identifiable character born in the early days of live television was the Old Gold Dancing Pack. Primitive but beguiling, the Old Gold ads featured a female dancer hidden inside a prop package of cigarettes. Her shapely legs, tapering down to a pair of white cowboy boots, tap-danced to "Sidewalks of New York." She was often accompanied by a second girl inside a matchbox, and later she was joined by a taller Old Gold King Size cigarette box, sporting a statuesque pair of legs. The Dancing Pack tapped her way through such shows as *Stop the Music* and *The Original Amateur Hour* and became one of the most familiar sights on early TV.

Connoisseurs of TV commercials often rate happy, sprightly "Speedy" Alka-Seltzer as the "purest" of the early identifiable characters. He was molded from the sponsor's product: Speedy's torso and cap were both Alka-Seltzer tablets. Designed by artist Robert Watkins for a 1952 magazine ad, Speedy was first brought to life in 1958 by Swift-Chaplin Productions in Hollywood, using the "pixilation" technique. In pixilation, a doll with movable joints is repositioned slightly with each exposed frame of motion picture film, lending an illusion of movement when the film is run. Speedy sang and played his toy piano and bongo drums. Waving his magic wand, Speedy cheerfully lectured viewers on the proper way to defeat "nasty old colds" until 1964, when he was taken off the air.

A strange fate awaited Speedy. He was lost in 1971 while being shipped to the Philippines. Wells, Rich & Green, the agency for Miles Laboratories that had replaced Wade Advertising, creator of Speedy, had to craft a new doll when

Also in 1948, the commercials for Ajax, "the Foaming Cleanser," entertained millions and expanded the potential of TV advertising with the first animated identifiable characters, the Ajax Pixies. These little elves—the tallest was three inches high—were cartoon figures, although they often interacted with live-action humans. "Pixies" was a commercial of "firsts." It was the first fully animated commercial of professional quality; the first work by the Shamus Culhane Studio, which was to dominate animated-commercial production through the early 1950s; and it was the first ad to introduce a popular TV commercial jingle. The country sang to: "You'll stop paying the 'elbow tax,' when you start cleaning with Ajax . . ."

The original Old Gold Dancing Pack, *left,* is joined by her sister, Old Gold King Size. The Old Gold Pack appeared ''live'' at least four nights a week during the early fifties. (MCA Advertising, 1953)

For years, Friskies dog food was pitched by a suave canine master of ceremonies, who sported a bow tie and boutonniere, and his mischievous assistant. (Erwin Wasey, circa 1955)

Miles Laboratories brought Speedy back to celebrate the nation's Bicentennial. Here he is from the 1976 commercial, singing, ''Plop, plop, fizz, fizz.'' His baton became an umbrella to protect him from Alka-Seltzer's effervescence. (Wells, Rich, Greene, 1976)

they revived the pixie for the U.S. Bicentennial. The new commercial celebrated Speedy as a national treasure. For the first time, viewers were able to see Speedy in color, with red hair and blue eyes, as he sang, "Plop, plop, fizz, fizz, oh, what a relief it is!" However, Speedy looked "different." Then, in 1979, the original Speedy was discovered, along with his little piano and miniature bongo drums, in an Australian warehouse. In one of show business's great comebacks, he starred in a pair of commercials aired during the 1980 Winter Olympics. Until his next appearance, Speedy Alka-Seltzer stands patiently in a glass case, greeting visitors to the Miles Laboratories in Elkhart, Indiana.

THE EARLY ANIMAL IDs

Animals were recognized early on by advertisers for their potential as identifiable characters. Not only did such logical sponsors as Friskies dog food introduce animal IDs in the fifties, but unlikely companies, such as Lyon Moving and Storage, used animal IDs because they were "cute." The most memorable automobile commercials of that time employed a cartoon dog. The Ford Dog was a whimsical departure in automotive advertising, when most car commercials consisted of running shots of the latest models cruising along highways. The coup was enjoyed by the J. Walter Thompson agency, for decades the nation's largest advertising firm. *Time* magazine, forgetting that the agency's principal client was Ford, once referred to JWT as "the Cadillac of the advertising business." But most of the credit belonged to a Hollywood animator named Adrian Woolery. Launching his own studio, Playhouse Pictures, which would become one of the top cartoon commercial houses during the fifties, Woolery brought some of his sketches of the shaggy, floppy-eared dog to Detroit. Ford found the dog appealing, and so did viewers when he first began cavorting around new cars in 1952. The advertisers later put the dog in the driver's seat!

A simple hand puppet was used as an identifiable character for this 1952 Lyon Moving and Storage Company ad. With his spiky whiskers and ears resembling a telephone mouthpiece, Leo Lion was outfitted in the company's uniform from the days when moving men wore caps and bow ties. (Direct, 1952)

The Ford Dog drove a car shaped like the Ford logo. He was also the first ID character to inspire merchandising spin-offs, such as the Ford Dog doll bank. (J. Walter Thompson, 1952)

Sharpie, the Gillette parrot, stepped up to the plate and later advised a teammate about Blue Blades. As the march cadences of the Gillette jingle played ''Look Sharp! Feel Sharp! Be Sharp!'' Sharpie mugged his way through commercials that were shown during wrestling matches, prizefights, and baseball games. (Maxen Agency, 1952)

The Clydesdales pull Budweiser's turn-of-the-century beer wagon. Symbols for the Anheuser-Busch Brewery for decades, the team has been appearing in commercials since 1951. (D'Arcy McManus & Masius, 1970)

Sharpie, the Gillette parrot, also made his debut in 1952. He appeared on the first World Series broadcast and was seen as many as eight times a night during boxing matches and sporting events sponsored by the Boston-based Gillette Company until 1960. Created by the Maxen Agency as an appealing way to hawk Blue Blades, Sharpie was first drawn as a simple white-line silhouette against a black backdrop. His animated antics were then superimposed over live pictures of a baseball diamond or a boxing arena. Later he was fully animated and appeared in sixty-second comedies accompanied by the tuneful "To Look Sharp" jingle. Promising "the quickest, slickest shave of all," the song was composed to a march tempo, and Sharpie, who never spoke, would often conduct. "Look Sharp! Feel Sharp! Be Sharp!" The popular jingle became so closely identified with sporting events that high school and college marching bands still perform it at games today.

Often it seems that God must have created the Clydesdale horse to advertise Budweiser, so closely has the animal become associated with the "King of Beers." The Anheuser-Busch Company of St. Louis introduced the Clydesdales to TV in 1951. Anheuser-Busch is one of the world's largest breweries and is the world's largest breeder of Clydesdales. In Budweiser's first TV ad, the D'Arcy McManus & Masius agency photographed a team of eight horses pulling Budweiser's trademark wagon through the gates of the August Busch estate built by Ulysses S. Grant's father. Budweiser has been with the D'Arcy McManus & Masius agency since 1915, certainly some type of longevity record in the revolving-door world of client–ad agency relations.

The Clydesdale hitch has been seen in commercials for over thirty years and has also become a staple of parades all over the country. Like the three Goodyear blimps that are moored in different locations around the country, Clydesdale hitches are housed in St. Louis, Missouri, Valencia, California, and Merrimack, New Hampshire. The enduring Clydesdale symbol was even employed to introduce Bud Light beer in 1982. Filmed in slow motion, a single Clydesdale galloped through snow and stream, kicking up spray, and appeared remarkably lightfooted for such an imposing animal.

PARADE OF ANIMATED IDs

The art of animation in television commercials reached its zenith during the fifties. This was partly a result of economics. Live commercials were replaced by filmed ads, which were expensive to produce. Animation was cheaper. But animation was really successful because viewers demanded novel commercials; animation was capable of imaginatively restructuring reality, and viewers responded to its techniques.

The standards of innovative animation were set by the UPA studio (United Producers of America), founded by disgruntled Walt Disney cartoonists in 1943. UPA's most successful venture into commercials was with a pair of bumbling businessman brothers, Bert and Harry Piel.

Bert and Harry Piel "aim to please." New Yorkers were devoted fans of the Piels' antics and would eagerly await each week's new installment. (Young & Rubicam, 1953)

The Piel Brothers, the fictitious owners of the Piel's brewery, inspired such an amazing viewer response during the mid-fifties that the only comparable broadcasting precedent was the *Amos 'n' Andy* radio show.

Bert and Harry appeared solely in a local market to sell a local product—New York State's Piel's Beer—but this did not prevent them from gaining national fame.

Bert and Harry were custom-designed for the comedy team of Bob and Ray. Bob Elliot and Ray Goulding had performed their low-key brand of social satire and media spoofs on radio and early TV, and they managed to translate their humor effortlessly into the Piel's animated commercials. The UPA studio employed a clean, simple, black-and-white line-drawing style to depict cartoon characters that complemented Bob and Ray's voices. Loudmouthed, pompous Bert Piel and quiet, befuddled Harry—together they would stumble through their slapstick sales pitches while, at the same time, they mocked the conventions of theatrical illusion. The brothers would call for camera shots, yell stage directions, and similarly unmask the mechanics of filmmaking. "Say, that's real drinking pleasure, isn't it, viewers?" Bert would proclaim. "And . . . wait a minute! I asked for a *close-up* shot of the label of our twelve-ounce bottle!"

Bert and Harry ran from 1951 until 1960. New Yorkers grieved at their absence. In 1962, viewers were polled to see if the duo should return. Buoyed by thousands of positive responses, Bert and Harry came back to broadcast their brewery antics until 1965. They returned once again to make a nostalgic appearance during the mid-seventies.

John Hubley's commercial studio, Storyboard Productions, was responsible for Wally—a big-beaked, champagne-sipping cartoon bird who has been advising televiewers since the mid-fifties that Western Airlines is the *ooonly* way to fly. Wally's name is an anagram derived from the words "Western Airlines Loves You": W-AL-L-Y.

One of Hollywood's top commercial directors, John Urie, recalls the birth of Wally: "I was an assistant animator at Storyboard, which had just produced some fabulously successful campaigns, like 'It's a F-O-R-D!' and Speedway Gasoline. But Hubley threw the Western Airlines assignment out to everyone for ideas. I thought, why not have a bird, a talking bird, that hitches a ride on top of a plane? This bird tells a friend that it's the best way to fly. 'Take it from an expert' sort of thing. It's simple logic."

"I drew a picture and showed it to Hubley. He liked it and we had a brainstorming session, trying to figure out what this bird should say, something like 'It's the way to fly.' Hubley's partner, Les Goldman, walked by and said in a deep voice, 'It's the *ooonly* way to fly!' We knew we had it."

Hitching a luxury ride atop a Western Airlines plane of the fifties, Wally proclaimed the champagne service "The *oonly* way to fly"—a slogan that became one of commercials' most repeated lines. (Buchanan Advertising, 1955)

The Hamm's Bear leads his friends through the "land of sky-blue waters." (Campbell-Mithun, 1965)

Wally was Urie's big break in the business. He would go on to direct thousands of commercials and set up John Urie and Associates, one of the top commercial production houses during the sixties. Meanwhile, Wally continued to hitch rides up and down the West Coast on Western, his popularity undiminished in subsequent years. Jets have replaced the old propeller-driven Constellations, but Wally's ads have not changed since 1955.

Another animated ID is the Hamm's Bear. His slapstick antics were enjoyed for years only by viewers in the Midwest, where Hamm's beer, brewed "in the land of sky-blue waters" on Minnehaha Street in St. Paul, was distributed. The bumbling Hamm's Bear would frolic around the woods and the ten thousand lakes of Minnesota, having misadventures with his animal companions. When he would fish with his best buddy, Big Moose, the Bear would end up playing tug-of-war for control of the fishing line with his own reflection in the water. Of course, the Bear would lose and get pulled into the pool. When he would try to act with dignity, running for mayor of the forest or conducting the Woodland Symphony Orchestra, the Bear would be pummeled with acorns thrown by the mischievous Raccoon Twins. Starting in 1955, the Bear appeared in more than one hundred commercials—the commercials were always accompanied by the beating of tomtom drums that began the Hamm's jingle: "From the Land of sky-blue water/Land of lake and pine . . ."

In the mid-sixties, the animated Bear be-

gan to appear in live-action ads. He also acquired a voice with which to say his one and only line: "It *bears* repeating." Heublein, Inc., acquired the brewery in 1968 and retired the bear. He hibernated for ten years, until the conglomerate sold Hamm's to the Olympia Brewing Company ("It's the water!"). With Olympia's expansive distribution network, Hamm's Beer was made available in twenty-five states. The Bear made his reappearance in his first national commercials in 1978, still mugging it up. For the Bear's twenty-fifth birthday celebration, in 1980, an actor costumed as the Bear sliced up a fourteen-foot-high bear-shaped cake confected by students at St. Paul's Technical Vocational Institute. Yogi and Boo Boo Bear from Jellystone National Park showed up at the party, which was held at St. Paul's Como Park Zoo. As thousands cheered, the city's mayor gave the Hamm's Bear a plaque honoring the brewery for its gifts to the zoo over the years: a grizzly and a polar bear, both gifts inspired by Hamm's engaging identifiable bruin.

Another beer, Carling's Black Label, a Canadian brew, was identified for years in the fifties with an attractive waitress named Mabel. Actress Jean Davis started portraying Mabel in 1951. When she left to have a child, Carling's agency decided to replace her with an animated character. The cartoon Mabel would always be on hand to answer the whistle or calls of bar patrons. "Hey Mabel, Black Label!" became such a popular jingle that a full-length version appeared in jukeboxes around the nation.

WHAT'S HER NAME?

Animation also proved to be the right format for bringing the Campbell Kids to television. Though the Kids seem inarguable treasures of Americana today, at one time they were endangered trademarks. Drawn by Philadelphia illustrator Grace Widerseim in 1904, the Kids were dimpled, pugnosed, and fat. "I made them chubby because I was a chubby child myself, and happy!" Widerseim said at the time. Her creations became as familiar as Campbell Soup's red-and-white labels until the economic imperatives of the Great Depression replaced whimsical advertising with the hard sell. However, the dimpled cherubs seemed ideally suited for postwar TV, and they were brought back in 1953 to sing, "M'm, M'm good/ M'm, M'm good, that's what Campbell's Soups are/ M'm, M'm good!" on *Lassie*. Outfitted in updated clothes, and slimmed down some, the Kids were seen as animated dolls similar to Speedy Alka-Seltzer. They instructed young viewers in good manners and proper nutrition. Considered too old-fashioned in the sixties, they disappeared once more, later to be revived yet again during the nostalgia craze of the seventies. The little tykes were put on a rigorous diet when Campbell's sponsored the U.S. figure-skating team in 1982. Currently seen in brief cartoon segments that begin Campbell's live-action soup commercials, the Kids still dispense cute aphorisms like: "Sunshine all around us/Campbell's when we're through/No wonder we just sparkle/At everything we do!"

One of the kings of animated commercials, Tony® the Tiger, has grown during his first thirty years. Once a fixture of children's television, he is now the "father figure" of all Kellogg's ID characters. He has proclaimed "They're GR-R-REAT!™" about Frosted Flakes® cereal since his 1955 debut. As originally designed by Martin Provensen, an illustrator of children's books, Tony looked considerably different in his early days: he was thinner, flatter, and had a head shaped like a football. Also, he at first was only as tall as his image appears (about seven or eight inches) on the cereal box, out of which he popped during his commercials. Tony's first appearances also featured a child tiger, addressed at first as "boy" and years later as "son." By the time of the adoption, Tony had grown to six and a half feet tall, dwarfing the live-action humans he now appeared with.

During the early sixties, he was seen in slapstick situations that are still some of the most sophisticated usages of rotoscoping, a process that combines cartoons with live action. Tony falls out of an airplane in one story and bounces off some skydivers' parachutes. In another, he falls into a tank at Marineland in Los Angeles and is picked up by a dolphin, who carries the terrified tiger through a flaming hoop.

The comedic situations became subtler during the seventies—Tony was a family man now, with a wife, a doting mother, and a new baby girl. Tony Jr.® was off on his own, promoting Frosted Rice® cereal. In the 1970s, Tony began to be seen on prime-time television in corporate ads, such as the annual Christmas commercial that features the entire Kellogg's stock company of ID characters. Tony is the king of the clan.

Tony the Tiger, the father figure to all of Kellogg's cereals' identifiable characters. Over the years, Tony has undergone a change of appearance and has acquired an entire family of tigers, including a son, Tony Jr., who pitched Kellogg's Frosted Rice in the first instance of identifiable-character nepotism. (Leo Burnett, 1975)

Snap!® Crackle!® and Pop!® also appeared in Kellogg's televised Christmas cards. Originally designed by another illustrator of children's books, W. T. Grant, they were three large-eared elves until Don Keller at Kellogg's agency, Leo Burnett of Chicago, and Quartet Film's Charles Mackelmurry "softened" their images to what we know today. Tony the Tiger has a distinctive personality enhanced by the growling bass voice of actor Thurel Ravenscroft, but neither Snap! Crackle! nor Pop! has a strong individual identity: One cannot tell them apart except for their hair color and costumes. And without strong character traits, comic invention is limited. The whimsical trio usually scampers around the kitchen, amusing youngsters by pointing out the famous aural features of Rice Krispies,® Frosted Rice, and Cocoa Krispies.® Snap! Crackle! and Pop! have endured for thirty years because they personify those noisy breakfast sounds heard whenever the cereal is doused with milk. And like all successful ID characters, they have become as familiar as old friends.

IDs OF THE SIXTIES: FANTASIES AND FRIENDS

Screwball fantasy situation comedies were in vogue on television in the mid-1960s. There was the best friend who was a talking horse, the wife who was a witch, the uncle who was a Martian, and the mother who was a car. Con-

During the era of fantasy programs on television, the mid- and late-sixties, commercials also produced a host of bizarre characters. The most exotic was the Ajax White Knight. (Ted Bates, 1969)

sidering the times, it was perhaps not unusual that one of the most popular identifiable characters was the Ajax White Knight. The White Knight symbolized the cleaning power of Ajax laundry detergent. By charging up suburban streets on his white steed and zapping soiled citizens with a dazzling ray emanating from his lance, he made their dirty clothes sparkle like new. Like Procter & Gamble's Mr. Clean, the Ajax White Knight was a strong, helpful, masculine figure ready to aid the beleaguered housewife with her chores. How strong was he? According to the baritone male chorus that sang his praises, the Ajax White Knight was "stronger than dirt!"

One of the friendliest, if most fantastic, of identifiable characters remains Poppin' Fresh, the beloved Pillsbury Doughboy. He was "born" at the Leo Burnett Agency in Chicago, like the Jolly Green Giant and the Marlboro Man. Rudi Perz, who created Poppin' Fresh, recalls how he was invented: "We had just landed the refrigerated dough business from Pillsbury [in 1966], and I had to come up with a campaign. In those days the directions on the package told the user to hit the tube against the edge of a counter. The package would break open and dough would pop out between the seams. I wondered what would happen if someone

Snap! Crackle! and Pop!, Kellogg's trio of cute and enduring elves. The three have remained active since the fifties, though none can boast of a distinctive personality. They are a true team, indistinguishable and indivisible. (Leo Burnett, 1978)

would pop out of the package along with the dough. He would be made of dough. The name 'Doughboy' naturally suggested itself.

"I discussed the idea with Leo Burnett. He felt an additional word was needed in the Doughboy's name. Something descriptive. Something like 'fresh.' I thought about the Doughboy popping out of the package, and said, 'Well, what about Poppin' Fresh?' 'That's it! That's it!' Leo said. Well, a character has to be likable. So we gave the Doughboy a funny little giggle that makes you feel good. He'd blush when a little girl kissed him, and he was shy when taking a compliment."

Poppin' Fresh, the Pillsbury Dough-boy, waves hello. Emerging from a tube of the sponsor's refrigerated dough product at the beginning of each commercial, Poppin' Fresh was eager to help around the kitchen, but proved bashful when shown affection, such as his friends' irresistible urge to poke him in his doughy belly. (Leo Burnett, 1966)

Poppin' Fresh, the Pillsbury Dough-boy, gets "poked" by a boy's index finger. Viewers never realized that the human "hands" seen in these commercials were fakes, rubber rep-licas that were repositioned frame by frame as the stop-motion sequence was shot, giving the illusion of move-ment. (Leo Burnett, 1966)

SORRY Charlie

Charlie the Tuna seems unfazed by Star Kist's rejection note. But he keeps on trying, which explains much of his popularity. (Leo Burnett, 1970)

The Doughboy was also "human" enough to take a wife; in the mid-seventies, we were introduced to Mrs. Poppin' Fresh, who wore a bonnet instead of a chef's hat like her husband. But she smiled with the same flour-white dimples and blue button eyes.

Charlie the Tuna is another Leo Burnett agency creation. In more than eighty commercials since 1961, the "beatnik" fish with the beret and dark glasses has tried to demonstrate to the Star Kist fishermen that he has good taste. He has played tennis with an octopus, plucked on a harp, and studied old masters; but all the while, he has ignored the advice of his friend, another tuna: "Charlie, Star Kist doesn't want tuna with good taste. Star Kist wants tuna that tastes good!" Invariably, the message arrives printed on a note dangling from a fish hook: "Sorry, Charlie!"

Marv Greenberg, who works on the Star Kist account at Burnett, feels that tenacity is the key to Charlie's appeal. "He's got great resilience, and doesn't get too despondent. He keeps trying. But he's also an antihero. He's

street-smart. He knows that Star Kist is where all the great tunas go. But he's always exposed by what we call his 'Charlieisms.' For instance, his friend will swim by and ask him, 'What's the book about, Charlie?' And Charlie, whose voice is done by Herschel Bernardi, will answer, 'It's not about nothin'. It's poetry.' But he's not just a loudmouthed bore. There's a vulnerability about him. And Charlie's very enthusiastic."

No one would ever say Morris the Cat, yet another Leo Burnett creation, was enthusiastic. Though the fifteen-pound, orange-colored tabby with the bass voice insisted, "A cat who doesn't act finicky loses the respect of its master," he would finally yield and gobble up his dinner. Morris exemplified the independence that cat owners cherish in their pets. He would condescend to his master, a silly woman with an annoying, high-pitched voice. "Playing with yarn is stupid," he would tell viewers. "But cat owners expect it." Visiting a kennel in one commercial, the woman who "owns" Morris burbles, "Oh, look, Morris. Puppies! Aren't they cute?" "Silly, stupid, sloppy, maybe," sniffs Morris, "but not cute. Cats are cute." While trying to enjoy a day at the beach, Morris finds himself surrounded by sand walls and towers. "Look, Morris, I made you a sand castle!" the

lady gushes. "Good," the cat replies dryly. "Reserve the dungeon for yourself."

Viewer response was so great that Nine Lives had to hire Morris a secretary to answer fan mail and send out eight-by-ten glossies "autographed" with his paw print. He was greeted on *The Mike Douglas Show* by a standing ovation, and his life story, *Morris: An Intimate Biography*, was published in 1975. Readers learned all about the melodramatic origins of the future star who was "discovered" by animal trainer Bob Martwick in an animal shelter in Lombard, Illinois. Martwick was impressed by the cat's gumption. He seemed wholly indifferent to the indignity of the shelter. And he was to prove just as "cool" in the pressure cooker of motion-picture production. A nation mourned when Morris died in 1978 at age seventeen. Nine Lives attempted to reincarnate their inimitable spokescat in the early eighties with imitation tabbies, but to his fans, there will always be only one Morris.

There has never been an identifiable character quite like the gun-toting outlaw, the "friendly villain" known as the Frito Bandito. One of the most controversial identifiable characters, he promoted Frito's corn chips during the sixties. The Foote, Cone & Belding agency

An imperturbable Morris the Cat awaits his Nine Lives cat food. The finicky Morris was considered every cat owner's ideal pet, though he treated his own master with undisguised contempt. There was little that met with Morris's approval except, grudgingly, the sponsor's product. (Leo Burnett, 1969)

Frito Bandito, the smiling outlaw. (Foote, Cone & Belding, 1967)

of Chicago created the cartoon Pancho Villa look-alike, who held up supermarkets, pedestrians, picnickers, and anyone else who happened to carry his favorite snack. The "Muncha Buncha Fritos" jingle played at the conclusion of each ad as an actor or actress would sneak into a bag and steal some chips. When the announcer asked, "Is there a Frito Bandito in your house?" an animated mustache similar to the Bandito's curled across the perpetrator's lip.

Critics in the Mexican-American community charged that the Bandito was an offensive ethnic stereotype. The Houston-based Frito-Lay company was too prominent in the American Southwest to afford insensitivity. It commissioned a survey among Chicano consumers. While newspapers played up the story, pollsters found that only 8 percent of Mexican Americans disliked the Bandito. A predominantly Chicano junior high in San Antonio petitioned Frito-Lay, writing: "If you take our Bandito off the air, we'll stop buying your product."

Other identifiable characters were also under fire during this time. Some blacks objected to Uncle Ben, the servile waiter in the starched white coat who served up Uncle Ben's Converted Rice. He disappeared from all advertising, and was dropped from the product box. Aunt Jemima was redesigned from the familiar "mammy" character, making her slimmer and more youthful. But Frito-Lay stood firm. When the Frito Bandito finally packed up his yellow sombrero in the early seventies, he was retired because he was no longer selling as many chips as in his gunslinging prime.

The plaintive cry of a tiny, furry, sad-eyed, and big-eared koala was first heard across the land in 1967: "I Hate Qantas!" The Australian air carrier, virtually unknown in the U.S. before the bear made his appearance, was immediately perceived as a major airline. Viewers assumed that any company that would allow itself to be maligned in its own commercials must be large and confident.

The koala's first ad, "Up a Tree," ran for ten years, interspersed with other episodes. Filmed by Lee Lacy and Associates, this creation of the Cunningham & Walsh agency featured the little bear dangling lazily from a eucalyptus tree over the rippled surface of a pond. Forest noises, the chirping of birds and crickets, were heard in the background as he lamented sulkily: "Unbearable. That's what it is—unbearable. Australia is *crawling* with tourists. And I know who's to blame. I know. Qantas! That's who. Qantas! What a name for an airline!"

The little koala squinted into the sun. Overhead, a roaring 707 descended. "Every day. Every single day," he complained, and then sighed his signature slogan, "I hate Qantas!"

The original commercial of the series was filmed at the San Diego Zoo, home of some of the very few koalas that have been permitted to leave the Australian continent. The koala used for shooting was known locally as a civic mascot, and when he passed away, the citizens of San Diego gave him an informal civic funeral. Cunningham & Walsh opted thereafter to shoot its commercials "down under," where the supply of adorable koalas is endless. Qantas tripled its sales in the first nine years of the koala's existence, rivaling the major South Pacific carrier, Pan Am, though Qantas enjoyed only a fraction of Pan Am's advertising budget.

A sense of fantasy also pervaded the fast-paced, gag-filled Raid cartoon commercials of the late sixties and early seventies. Raid's ads had appeared before and after this period, but their high point was due to the contributions of Tex Avery, the veteran Hollywood animator who created Bugs Bunny and Daffy Duck. The character Captain Raid was invented by the Foote, Cone & Belding agency for the Johnson's Wax Company in 1957. The Captain—actually a silent, stern-faced can of insecticide—would use one brawny arm to push the aerosol button on top of his cap and, aiming at a rogue's gallery of comic insects, he would "kill bugs dead."

The most memorable commercials of the Captain's long career were six minute-long spots produced by Avery between 1968 and 1971. Each action-packed commercial followed the same plot line. Social undesirables, portrayed by bugs, would have their good times abruptly ended by the vengeful Captain Raid. In "Casino," the insects operate a speakeasy beneath the kitchen sink. "Place your bets!" shouts the croupier, and the bugs lay cupcakes atop a crap table made from a sardine tin.

The insecticide mist sprayed by the Captain would form into various shapes while destroying the vermin. In "Casino," the mist solidifies into a television set with the word *BOOM!* on its screen. "Hey! Picture, but no sound!" notes a roach. An instant later, the set explodes.

Two roach motorcycle punks terrorize a kitchen countertop in "Bugbikers." The Bugbikers fleeing Captain Raid find themselves atop a motorcycle fashioned from a cloud of spray. Another transformation changes the rear of the bike into a stack of dynamite and the front handlebars into a detonating plunger. *KABOOM!*

These Raid ads became the Roadrunner cartoons of commercials. The bugs, like Wile E. Coyote, would always come back for more mischief in the next episode.

ANIMAL IDs: THE SECOND GENERATION

Unlike their progenitors of two decades earlier, the identifiable animal characters of the seventies were far less entertaining, yet they fulfilled the more difficult function of representing firms whose services do not lend themselves to dramatics. The Hartford, for instance, distinguished itself among insurance companies by bringing to life a stag, its company trademark for more than a century.

The Dreyfus Corporation established itself on TV by presenting the startling sight of a full-grown lion emerging from the New York City subway. In the mid-sixties, the use of an identifiable character was a dramatic breakthrough for a money-market fund, the type of service usually advertised in gray "tombstone" newspaper ads. Jack Dreyfus, chairman of the

Captain Raid in action! A shot of insecticide spray from the nozzle atop his head "kills bugs dead." Knowing its commercials might be shown during the dinner hour, the sponsor, S. C. Johnson & Sons, opted for humorous animated commercials instead of film showing dying roaches. The gag-filled ads have changed little in a quarter-century. (Foote, Cone & Belding, 1970)

Since 1974, a ten-foot-tall stag (measured from hoof to the tip of his antler rack) by the name of Laurence has represented the Hartford. In his ads the stag, a live incarnation of the insurance company's symbol since the nineteenth century, wanders into suburban homes, businesses, and wherever the Hartford's coverage extends. (McCaffrey-McCall, 1977)

Major, the Dreyfus lion, prowls the Wall Street jungle. The lion was a dramatic innovation in the sixties. (Doyle Dane Bernbach, 1966)

Dreyfus Fund, had the idea of symbolizing the "dignity, power, and confidence" of his firm with a lion, "the king of the financial jungle." The Doyle Dane Bernbach agency re-created a section of Wall Street inside a Hollywood soundstage for the commercial; it showed a lion named Major strolling out of a subway entrance and past a newsstand and dozens of uninterested passersby (obviously jaded New Yorkers, who have seen stranger sights).

In 1982, Dreyfus's in-house ad agency, the 767 Agency (named after the address of its home, the General Motors Building at 767 Fifth Avenue in Manhattan), decided to bring back their symbol after a decade's retirement. The new ads used the original fifteen-year-old footage of Major, sepia-toned to lend a nostalgic feeling. Major was a "professional animal," raised by trainers expressly for filmmaking. He was as much at home under hot studio lights as he might have been under the African sun.

Like the Dreyfus lion, the Merrill Lynch bull has a name, too. He is Merrill. He is also a veteran movie actor and a living incarnation of the sponsor's trademark. The bull symbolizes the tenacity, size, and strength of the nation's largest brokerage house, Merrill Lynch, Pierce, Fenner and Smith. The Ogilvy & Mather agency followed its initial "Thundering Herd" ad of 1976, which featured a herd of bulls running against a sunset, with "Wall Street," Merrill's first solo appearance. In that ad, the Longhorn bull ran from the New York Stock Exchange on Bond Street, turned right at the statue of George Washington in front of the Federal Reserve, and charged toward the camera. During the filming of the commercial, however, Merrill was repeatedly spooked by the camera crew and kept running away, toward Trinity Church, until barricades were erected to herd him along.

Merrill's best performance was in the 1980 commercial "China Shop." The bull spent sixteen hours under blazing studio lights, negotiating cases filled with real crystal. It was an art director on the set who accidentally shattered a $3,500 Baccarat candelabrum, not Merrill. "China Shop," which showed the powerful but surefooted bull cautiously navigating the perils of his surroundings, was telecast when stocks were fluctuating. In this and subsequent commercials, Merrill acted like a pro, tolerating even the makeup crew that dyed him a photogenic shade of black. Of course, the bull was given star treatment—he even had a cow to keep him company on the set.

Merrill, the Merrill Lynch bull, is loose in a china shop. Unlike the crew, he broke nothing during the filming of the commercial. Merrill also is a living incarnation of his sponsor's trademark. (Young & Rubicam, 1980)

THE HUMAN IDs

Character actors have proved that their inventive personalities can be just as charming as animated or animal ID characters. Their popularity and longevity bear this out.

The Quaker Oats Company's most endearing identifiable character has been a sulky, brown-haired three-year-old named Mikey. His first appearance for Life cereal in 1972 began a success story that business classes use as a case study in profitable advertising campaigns. The key to Mikey's success, of course, is "personality."

Life cereal was created by Quaker as a nutritious breakfast food containing more "consumable protein" than any other cereal on the market. Since its introduction in the sixties, Life had suffered from uninspired hard-sell commercials featuring announcers armed with charts and graphs who lectured on nutritional claims. Doyle, Dane, Bernbach, working closely with Quaker, opted for a different approach. The resulting commercial, titled "Three Brothers," is based on "a real human experience," according to Quaker's vice-president, Elizabeth Harrington. "Few mothers have ever had a child who did not refuse to eat." Mikey is the youngest of three siblings, a little boy who "won't eat anything," as an older brother says. Suspicious of the new cereal "that's supposed to be good for you," the two older boys argue over which one will try it first. They decide to shove the bowl across the table to the freckle-faced Mikey. Astounding his brothers, Mikey gobbles up the Life without a word. The commercial struck a chord, and its popularity kept it on the air for a decade. "People ask us how we got Mikey to act," says Harrington. "But we didn't *get* Mikey to do anything. We let the children be themselves. If you really want a blockbuster ad with magic and charm, you create a situation in which children can be themselves—a natural, real-life situation."

As portrayed by Jane Withers, Josephine, the lady plumber, gives the thumbs-up. (Compton Advertising, 1965)

One character actress who discovered a second career in television commercials, Jane Withers, is as effervescent today as when she was Shirley Temple's rival as the movie's top child star of the thirties. Three decades later, having raised a family of five and having turned down offers to appear in thirty other commercials because she did not believe in the sponsor's products, Withers decided the time

BBDO
Batten, Barton, Durstine & Osborn, Inc.

Client: **QUAKER OATS CO.**		Time: **30 SECONDS**
Product: **LIFE CEREAL**	Title: **"THREE BROTHERS" REV.**	Comml. No.: **OAAL3664**

1ST BOY: What's this stuff?
2ND BOY: Some cereal. Supposed to be good for you.

1ST BOY: D'you try it?
2ND BOY: I'm not gonna' try it, you try it.

1ST BOY: I'm not gonna' try it.

2ND BOY: Let's get Mikey!
1ST BOY: Yeah!

2ND BOY: He won't eat it. He hates everything.

2ND BOY: He likes it!

Hey Mikey!
ANNCR: (VO) When you bring Life home, don't tell the kids it's one of those

nutritional cereals you've been trying to get them to eat. You're the only one who has to know.

The Maytag Repairman, "the loneliest man in town," fills his solitude by serenading his sad-eyed basset hound. (Leo Burnett, 1978)

was right to accept the role of spokeswoman for Comet Cleanser. Her main reason for going back to work was that her husband wanted to study law, and to support the family. She "loved the idea" of playing a lady plumber named Josephine.

"I spent twelve weeks learning the plumbing trade, preparing for the role. I went out with plumbers on their jobs, into people's homes. They'd look at me funny, and finally they'd say, 'Aren't you Jane Withers? I *thought* you looked familiar!' They were thrilled that I was learning the plumbing business in their homes. They would invite all the neighbors over, and we'd have a ball. Procter & Gamble, meanwhile, had no idea that I was doing this, and they were thrilled when they learned.

"The commercials were on the air for twelve and a half years. People really did love Josephine. I received thousands of letters. Hundreds were from my fans in French-speaking Canada, asking me why they didn't hear my voice in the French language versions of the Comet commercials. I told the agency people that I would gladly learn French Canadian,

and later we produced a separate series of commercials for that part of Canada in the proper dialect to make those sweet people happy. I cared that much about Josephine, and I've really tried to make people happy in everything I do."

Jesse White, the character actor who portrays the Maytag Repairman, also feels strongly about his creation: "I love the guy. He's so sweet. He's so *lonely*." Indeed, "the loneliest man in town" has been seen in commercials since 1967, waiting, sometimes patiently, sometimes not, for customers to call and request repairs for their Maytag washers. They never do. The woeful Maytag Repairman goes to a warehouse in one ad, and like a drill sergeant inspecting his troops, he addresses a line of washing machines. "Sure, you're dependable," he tells them. "But just once, can't you lose a screw? Break a drive belt? Anything! *Please*." Later in the series, the Repairman is called by a ghostly voice to fix a machine. He rows across a stormy sea and climbs a mountain to reach the job, but then he wakes up from what was, alas, "only a dream." He finally receives a legitimate service call; it takes him out to an isolated lighthouse perched atop a rocky island. "Why, it's just a broken plug. You could have repaired it yourself," he tells the lighthouse keeper. "I know," the other man replies. "But it gets so lonely here, too!" At this poignant moment, the Maytag Repairman realizes he has found a kindred soul.

Thanks to the sympathetic outpouring that has greeted the Repairman over the years, the small Maytag Company of Newton, Iowa, is perceived as a major-leaguer. Maytag has never enjoyed a substantial advertising budget. Appliance manufacturers traditionally keep their advertising costs low to reduce the prices of their "big ticket" machines; personal-product companies like Gillette take a different route and channel 30 to 40 percent of their gross earnings into advertising, packaging, and marketing. One of the reasons why the Maytag Repairman's commercials, which are really just one-gag stories, have remained popular is that the Repairman has not suffered from overexposure.

Jesse White is one of a quartet of character actors whose real-life identities have been supplanted in the public's mind with the memorable ID characters they have created. This small clique of friends, who all reside in Los Angeles, includes Jesse White; Jane Withers; Dick Wilson, known to televiewers as Mr. Whipple; and Virginia Christine, a.k.a. Mrs. Olsen. When they appear on TV talk shows together, always to a tumultuous ovation from the audience, the jokes fly. "I've known Dick Wilson all my life," testifies Jesse White. "And he hasn't changed. He's *always* looked old." And as far as

the public is concerned, Dick Wilson has always been Mr. Whipple, the nebbishy storekeeper who, over the years, has tried to keep customers from fondling his toilet paper. His cry, "Ladies, please don't squeeze the Charmin!" became one of commercials' most-quoted lines.

"I lost count after we did four or five hundred Charmin commercials," says Wilson, "but I remember the first one was shot at a market in Flushing, New York, in 1965. If you can imagine—a commercial for toilet paper shot in Flushing! I read the script, and this Whipple character was written as a pretty mean guy. He'd grab the Charmin out of the ladies' hands and say, 'Don't squeeze that!' I suggested that *I* start squeezing the Charmin myself, and get caught in the act.

Mr. Whipple cannot resist squeezing the Charmin. (Benton & Bowles, 1970)

"In one commercial we had a St. Bernard who was supposed to bark whenever someone squeezed the Charmin. But the dog wouldn't bark. I got it to bark, though. I stepped on his tail. But don't tell the ASPCA." In another commercial, Whipple trains a parrot to say, "Ladies, please don't squeeze the Charmin." The bird begins to flirt with the ladies instead of issuing his warning. "I pointed to the parrot and said, 'I'm not going to use you again!' And that's when it happened—the bird bit my finger clean through to the bone!" The freeze-frame expression of pain that ended that particular commercial, with Whipple's index finger caught in the parrot's beak, was genuine.

Wilson began his career as an acrobatic dancer in vaudeville. His work for Charmin's agency, Benton & Bowles, represents the longest continuously running campaign in TV commercial history. "And it couldn't have happened to a nicer guy," jokes Wilson. "People come up to me all the time and say, 'Hey, you're Mr. Whipple!' If you can believe it, they give me rolls of toilet paper to autograph! Most of the time I can't. 'That's not Charmin,' I have to tell them. The texture is wrong or it's too hard. After all these years of squeezing Charmin, I *know* what it feels like."

While Wilson and White clown on talk shows, Virginia Christine is always charming, and as Mrs. Olsen, she has come to personify neighborliness, care, and Old World charm. This was evident in her first black-and-white commercial in 1963 when she knocked on the door of a newlywed couple who were frantically moving into their new house and offered her assistance along with a jar of Folger's "Mountain Grown" coffee ("It's the richest kind!). Always on hand to stir the fondue, TV's first Scandinavian identifiable character also salvaged several marriages over the years by recommending Folger's to young wives whose husbands had insulted their coffee. In the pre-women's-lib days, doe-eyed wives would whimper when their husbands criticized their coffee. In more recent episodes, strong-willed wives look like they just might empty the contents of the coffeepot on their husbands' heads. By the end of the sixties, Mrs. Olsen became the most recognizable face in TV commercials.

Another recognizable group is the Fruit of the Loom characters, who made their debut on April 6, 1975. As conceived by Grey Advertising, the fruit quartet of black and green grapes, leaves, and an apple was supposed to appear in only one commercial, announcing a product price reduction. They were so well received, however, that Fruit of the Loom opted to keep them on the air.

"In their earliest form," recalls Lester Schwartz, vice-president of advertising for the Union Underwear Company of Bowling

Green, Kentucky, "the four fruit characters were more or less immobile as part of a giant replica of the Fruit of the Loom logo. This was attached to an oversized undershirt. The fruits could talk and move their arms, but little else." Outfits were finally developed that gave the fruits complete freedom of movement, and these became the most popular costumes on TV. Fruit of the Loom sent its quartet to appear at Mardi Gras, state and county fairs, local parades, and autograph sessions at shopping malls, where they were received as legitimate TV stars. Fans were given photos in-scribed with "Best Wishes from the Apple," "Greetings from the Grape," and similar fruity sentiments.

Also intended as a character for a one-shot commercial was Brother Dominic. Former Borscht Belt comedian Jack Eagle first por-trayed the Chubby little monk for Xerox in an ad created by the Needham, Harper & Steers agency in 1975. In his first commercial, he is complimented by his superior at the abbey for having laboriously copied an illuminated page by hand. He is then ordered to produce five hundred identical copies.

The happiest company logo. The Fruit of the Loom Fruit Quartet strikes a pose. Theirs are the most popular costumes in commercials. (Grey Advertising, 1980)

FRUIT OF THE LOOM®

"CHANGE PARTNERS"

30 SECONDS

FIDDLER: Change your partner . . .

ALL FRUIT: Change your underwear.
(SFX: BOING)

LEAF: (SINGS) Hey, you don't wear Fruit of the Loom®.

PURPLE GRAPE: (SINGS) But we can make you change your tune.

APPLE: (SINGS) If our Superband® waistband didn't get you . . .

LEAF: (SINGS) Our Super Seams will-- that we'll bet you.

GREEN GRAPE: (SINGS) They're improved and made real strong.

PURPLE GRAPE: (SINGS) That will make 'em last real long.

EMMA: (SINGS) And you can have 'em for a song.

FIDDLER: I'll change, partners.
ALL: (SING) Hee Haw.

FRUIT: Improved Fruit of the Loom® men's cotton briefs. Only $1.97.

For another great value, there's cotton and polyester Golden Blend™ underwear.

Brother Dominic is an underdog, a man put upon by his boss, and despite his exotic vocation, he creates a bond of understanding and sympathy with his viewers. Perhaps the first "empathetic" ID character, the monk is also unusual since he, a "gentle little man," is promoting a high-tech behemoth, the Xerox 9200 copier. In the commercial, Brother Dominic rushes into town and uses this machine to make his reproductions. Upon returning to the abbey, the monk presents his five hundred flawless copies to the abbot, who raises his eyes to heaven and murmurs, "It's a miracle!"

Brother Dominic has become a huge hit for the Stamford, Connecticut-based Xerox Corporation. Jack Eagle dresses up as the monk three hundred days a year for appearances at trade shows and conventions, and on TV talk shows. Although he was also seen as the villainous Mr. Cholesterol in the Fleishmann margarine ads of the mid-seventies, Eagle acknowledges that his real fame comes from his role as

Brother Dominic. "I'm like the RCA dog," he says. "There's only one of me!"

The same might be said for the other popular and inimitable identifiable characters that have stood the test of time to become trusted video companions. These are the dramatis personae of commercials, protagonists of small allegories whose morals are apparent. The fable of the Maytag Repairman might finish with the proverb: "Happy is the man, even though he be lonely, who stands behind a quality product." The story of Charlie the Tuna, the fish who wants to be caught and canned, is a cautionary tale about the self-destructive compulsion to be "in." Morris the Cat preaches the foolishness of false pride. And the good-neighbor Christianity of Josephine, Comet Cleanser's Lady Plumber, is manifest in Jane Withers's desire to project a Samaritan in her scripts. These characters are well-developed and genuine—that is the very reason for their initial and enduring appeal.

Brother Dominic raises his eyes to heaven, but relies on a secular power to assist him: the Xerox 9200 copier. He lends warmth and humanity to the sponsor's cold, often intimidating machine. (Needham, Harper & Steers, 1975)

Chapter Two

Women in Commercials

"Does or does

The "looking glass" of television is actually a funhouse mirror. Commercials create an ideal world, and so their "reflection" of society emphasizes the attractive and the desirable. TV viewers respond to this ideal and not only want to possess the products advertised, but wish to be *like* the people in the commercials. Actors and actresses live the

she...
n't she?"

charmed lives of fairy-tale characters whose problems are solved in sixty seconds or less. Viewers often envy these characters and covet their beauty, self-confidence, and self-satisfaction.

But while there is little doubt that commercials influence consumer behavior, it is the consumers themselves who determine the content of commercials. If the woman of the Eisenhower era was commonly found at home, doing her part for the Baby Boom, then that was where American business, and the media, placed her on television. At the same time, she was benevolently assisted in performing her duties by an array of beauty aids and kitchen appliances. During the sixties and seventies, women asserted their rights to independent lives and equality with their mates; accordingly, advertisers "liberated" them from the hearth and glamorized their new careers. Although few advertisers are bold enough to predict trends—the nature of commercial-making being innately conservative, since it is so costly—no one dares be behind the times.

Advertisers are not in the business of perpetuating sexual myths. They are in the business of selling products, and women consumers essentially control the nation's purse strings. Yet, the majority of past television commercials have, been clearly sexist in their portrayals of women. With some notable real-life exceptions however, virtually *everyone* is stereotyped in commercials. As we shall see in a subsequent chapter, men have been subject to sterotyping also.

COMMERCIAL WOMEN OF THE FIFTIES: MOTHER AND HAUSFRAU

Some of the creations of popular culture from the fifties still retain their vitality. Kids still dance to Elvis, and *I Love Lucy* is timeless. But the pop art of commercials has not aged so gracefully. Consider the astonishment of the modern viewer who might turn on the tube and see the popular "Family Wash Blues" commercial that advertised the Bendix Duomatic washer/dryer in the mid-fifties. Like all good commercials, this one was wittily scripted and intelligently crafted. But its message about women is archaic. The first half-minute features a young housewife "drudge" in a shadowy dungeon of a basement. Singing a parody of Tennessee Ernie Ford's hit of the day about coal mining, "Sixteen Tons," she laments: "You wash sixteen tons, what do you get? . . ."

The scene shifts to a brightly lit set with a fashionably dressed woman literally pirouetting with joy beside her new washer/dryer. She sings: "You won't find me washing or drying clothes on the line/With my Bendix Duomatic my time is all mine . . ." Her time to do *what*?

**Drudge sings ''Family Wash Blues''
(Wade, 1955)**

**''Liberated'' by her Bendix washer/dryer, the woman goes shopping.
(Wade, 1955)**

Like all fifties "miracle" appliances, the Duomatic freed housewives from backbreaking work, but it was implied that their newly expanded free time would be spent on familial duties or frivolity. Carrying a large purse and wearing a Mamie Eisenhower-style pillbox hat, it was clear that the Bendix heroine was going shopping. And off she went, twirling away, but not before *blowing a kiss* to her washer/dryer.

Not all commercials of this era seem patronizing today. Pet Milk ran the same Christmas ad, called "Lullaby," from 1952 to 1959. It was one of the most unaffected ads ever broadcast, and, for viewers, one of the most emotionally touching. Perhaps the first cinema verité commercial, it was composed of a single shot, two minutes in length, of a young mother and her baby. As Brahms's "Lullaby" plays, she fondles her infant. The baby in turn pokes its mother in the eye and sticks its finger in her mouth with a spontaneity that saves the ad from sentimentality. Never has maternal love been better presented. The announcer's tag line over the concluding shot of a Pet Evaporated Milk can is a simple and dignified holiday greeting.

One imaginative variation on the proverbial theme, "A man may work from sun to sun,

Pet Evaporated Milk featured this mother and child every Christmas from 1952 through 1959. (Gardner, 1952)

but a woman's work is never done," was a humorous 1954 ad entitled "Busy Day." The inimitable *New Yorker* cartoonist Saul Steinberg was induced by the Young & Rubicam agency to draw the pictures for an animated commercial to introduce Jell-O's new instant pudding.

Done in Steinberg's unique style, the activities of a "harried housewife" are seen in a cutaway view of her head. Scenes of her cleaning the house, chasing the kids, and running errands are played out in different sections of her brain. These vignettes add up to a potential case of nervous exhaustion; the modern domestic world is increasingly demanding. The commercial offers a solution, though: a dessert that can be made instantly. Convenience foods such as these would proliferate until the "busy days" filled with burdensome household chores would become considerably lightened, leaving women to pursue other activities, such as careers, and paving the way for social changes that would be addressed in future commercials.

THE SPOKESWOMEN OF THE FIFTIES

The strongest and most credible female figures in the commercials of the fifties were spokeswomen, like Dinah Shore for Chevrolet, Betty Furness for Westinghouse refrigerators, and Polly Bergen for Pepsi. Ms. Shore never actually pitched Chevies on her top-rated Sunday-night variety show—women, after all, were not supposed to know anything about cars in those days. But Shore did help make her sponsor's automobile appear as much a national institution as baseball and hot dogs. Just before blowing her signature good-night kiss to her viewers, Dinah Shore ended each show with the classic jingle: "See the U.S.A. in your Chevrolet..."

Displaying the cornucopia of the fifties, Betty Furness was the decade's most trusted spokeswoman. (Ketchum, 1952)

Women were, however, granted license to speak about machines if these were parked in the kitchen. No spokesperson claimed higher credibility than Betty Furness. A slogan like "You Can Be Sure If It's Westinghouse" can backfire if the sarcastic viewer asks, "Sure about *what?*" But it never did. Furness preached the assurances of dependability and quality in the Westinghouse refrigerator/freezers whose doors she endlessly opened and closed during the decade, exposing prop milk cartons and papier-mâché roasts inside. These amply stocked refrigerators were the cornucopias of the fifties, symbolizing the nation's prosperity. Furness first became associated with the events of the era when the former model performed live Westinghouse commercials during the Republican and Democratic conventions of 1952 in Chicago. This was television's first coverage of the national conventions, and the immediacy of "gavel to gavel" coverage transfixed viewers. The many appearances of the indefatigable Furness with her white-enameled refrigerator marked the birth of a star. Two decades later, the Westinghouse spokeswoman would combine politics and consumerism once again when she was appointed to the New York Bureau of Consumer Affairs. By this time she was also a consumer reporter for NBC.

The ideal woman of the fifties was personified by Betty Crocker, the fictional "real life" identifiable character. Unlike most ID characters, which are the inventions of ad agencies, Betty Crocker was created in 1921 at the Westburn Crosby Company of Minneapolis, the forerunner of General Mills. Named after the company's director, William Crocker, "Betty" became familiar to radio listeners over Minneapolis's WLAG in 1924, and then over the National Broadcasting Company's airwaves in 1927. It was on NBC radio that she first presented her "I want to help" philosophy by explaining baking recipes. She elaborated this philosophy in verse during her television commercials from 1950 to 1960:

> *American homemakers*
> *Keepers of the hearth*
> *Whose hands and hearts are filled*
> *With the day-to-day cares and joys*
> *That, taken with one another,*
> *Make homemaking a woman's*
> *Most rewarding life.*

This message was first heard on *The Betty Crocker Television Show*, which aired over CBS in 1950 and 1951. The show was virtually a half-hour TV commercial. Also in 1951, Betty

The homemaker apotheosized: Betty Crocker displays one of her frosty confections. Along with baking recipes, she would dispense helpful hints and homey advice. (BBD&O, 1952)

Crocker, portrayed by actress Adelaide Hawley, performed in CBS's first color television commercial, where she concocted a "mystery fruitcake." She also baked up confections on two ABC daytime shows in 1952, *Betty Crocker Star Matinee* and *Bride and Groom*. In the latter show, she interviewed newlyweds back from their honeymoons and coached the brides on the preparation of their husbands' favorite dishes. Through the remainder of the decade, Adelaide Hawley appeared in chatty TV ads, greeting viewers brightly: "Hello, everybody! Once again, it's time for us to talk about 'something different' to help you drive that old mon-ster, monotony, right out your kitchen window." Beginning in 1955, she awarded the annual "Homemaker of Tomorrow" scholarship, and no one questioned the validity of sending a young worthy to college to become a better homemaker. Betty Crocker's popularity and credibility were enormous; 97 percent of American housewives recognized her by sight. Cheerful, helpful, friendly, she was a mature but companionable presence in the often lonely domestic reality of female viewers. Josephine the Lady Plumber and Mrs. Olsen, two other "household experts," would have much the same appeal a decade later.

The helpless heroine: In this sequence from the popular Bardahl ads of the fifties, an imperiled female motorist reacts to the image in her rearview mirror. He is engine trouble personified—a thug named Gummy Rings. (Direct, 1955)

HELPLESS HEROINES

The "damsel in distress" theme was the basis for the popular animated Bardahl series of the fifties. Bardahl, a detective type in a trench coat, whose eyes were hidden in the shadow of his snap-brim fedora, personified Bardahl motor oils and lubricants. He would rush to the aid of imperiled female motorists, usually beautiful, helpless blondes who were threatened by a gang of cutthroats: the gangster Blackie Carbon, who appeared inside the car's engine and choked the exhaust with his cigar smoke; Gummy Rings, a masked giant who sabotaged the car's piston rings; and Sticky Valves, whose machine gun sprayed noxious goo. Black activists in the sixties protested against the character of Blackie Carbon, who was not black, but rather an Edward G. Robinson lookalike. His name was changed to Crusty Carbon.

The commercials were *Dragnet* spoofs, with Bardahl narrating in Joe Friday's deadpan style the plight of the lady motorists at the hands of the trio of fiends. Rushing to the rescue, he would flush the villains out of the engine with a quart of motor oil. "Jeez! Let's beat it!" they would shout. "It's Bardahl!" A double-entendre gag ended each ad. Standing by the smooth-running auto, but obviously referring to the kittenish blonde snuggling up to him, Bardahl would say, "She's running nicely now. Listen to her purr!" Though the original Bardahl commercials of the fifties would not make it on American television today, they can still be seen in South America, where the tough, tight-lipped man and the frail, helpless woman are still acceptable caricatures.

Bardahl saves the day by adding motor oil to the engine and transforming the villain into a masked ghost. Women were not supposed to know anything about cars in the fifties. Reassuring, masculine identifiable characters like Bardahl promised freedom from worry. (Direct, 1955)

Goodyear's "Foggy Road" commercial in 1963 also played on the helplessness of the "weaker sex." It evoked all the fear and suspense of good Hitchcock. The story begins with a close-up of a tire blowout, with attention-grabbing sound effects. A woman driver steps out of her stranded car to find herself on a fogbound rural road, miles from anywhere. Her anxiety when she inspects the flattened tire turns to fear as she realizes her predicament. Says an announcer gravely: "When there's no man around—Goodyear should be." The chilling, theatrically produced commercial was directed by John Urie, who feels it is memorable because "it deals with emotions and really plays on fear." But its theme, the director adds, is that this is a man's world. Women can't take care of themselves or a car. You have to protect your woman by purchasing tires for her so she won't be accosted . . ."

Goodyear was promoting its innovative but expensive Double Eagle, a "tire within a tire." When the outer tire blew on this model, the inner "Lifeguard safety spare" kept right on spinning. Finding interesting ways to sell tires is always challenging, and the sponsor managed to follow "Foggy Road" with a 1964 sequel, "Phone Booth." The ad is a similar story: The imperiled female driver must hike from her car down a wet road late at night to phone for help. Both ads appear sexist by today's standards. Patronizingly, the announcer concludes each ad, "Next time, give her a second chance." A subtle marketing psychology was at work here, however. Women did not buy tires in 1963; men did. And it was men's ignorance about tires, not women's, that the commercials sought to overcome. "You see, men claim to know all about tires, but most don't," explains John Kelly, vice-president of advertising at the Goodyear Tire and Rubber Company in Akron, Ohio. "The explanations telling how the Double Eagle works were supposedly for women's benefit, but they were actually intended to educate men." Unfortunately for the sponsor, the commercials were unable to educate the thousands of gas-station atttendants who found it difficult to properly inflate the Double Eagle, and Goodyear's "tire within a tire" was discontinued.

FRIENDLY CONFIDANTES: KATY AND MADGE

Sympathetic female characters cast in confidential "woman to woman" commercials were one device used by sponsors to address the sensitive topic of feminine hygiene. Procter & Gamble featured Katy Winters as a "friend in need" in the mid-sixties. Flustered girlfriends with "perspiration problems" were advised in sixty-second dramas to keep "cool, calm, and collected" with Ice Blue Secret deodorant. Winters, a personable woman who was invariably cool, calm, and collected herself, saved many of her friends from embarrassment.

Katy Winters's appearances in these commercials were shortlived, but her contemporary, Madge the Manicurist, still advises her customers that "Palmolive softens hands while you do dishes." Madge, played by Jan Miner, is a wisecracking professional whose appeal has become international. In Germany, Austria, and Switzerland, she is " Tilly the Manicurist"; in France, "Françoise the Manicurist." Madge's scripts, written by the Ted Bates agency, have been the same since 1966. After commenting ironically on the dryness of her customers' hands and hearing their predictable reply, "It's dishwashing, Madge!" the manicurist reveals, while they sit at a table in the beauty salon, that her customers' fingers are just now soaking in dishwashing liquid. The cry goes out, "Dishwashing liquid!" and the hand recoils, only to be gently pushed back into the emerald-green Palmolive. Madge, despite her occasional acerbity, has an ability to make women believe her.

DOES SHE OR DOESN'T SHE?

In the sixties, women started entering the corporate world, and their influence in the advertising profession changed the content of commercials. It was symptomatic of the changing roles of women in American society that the values and fantasies of women were captured for the first time with fidelity by one of the first women to break into the creative ranks of advertising—Shirley Polykoff.

Ms. Polykoff is one of the only women in Washington, D.C.'s Advertising Hall of Fame. She is also the creator of the Clairol ads, which have changed the way women perceive themselves. Prior to 1955, only adventurous women like Polykoff dared dye their hair. She recalls, "If a woman got a gray hair, she'd pull it out. You could end up looking like Mahatma Gandhi." Miss Clairol Hair Conditioning sought to break through women's doubts about the "artificial look" of dyed hair. Polykoff sat in her office, at the Foote, Cone & Belding agency in Chicago, mulling over possible approaches for getting the message across. She recalled her first meeting with her mother-in-law, the immigrant wife of an Orthodox rabbi. The woman looked closely at Shirley's blond hair, then asked her son: *"Zee paint dos heur? Odder zee paint does nicht?"* Paraphrasing her mother-in-law's Yiddish, Polykoff created the slogan, "Does she, or doesn't she . . ." The question was answered, "only her mother knows for sure." However, as a sop to hairdressers, who were nervous about the first home hair dye and who might boycott other Clairol products, the line was changed to the now familiar, "Hair coloring

Ted Bates Advertising/New York

Client: COLGATE-PALMOLIVE CO.
Product: PALMOLIVE LIQUID
Comm'l No.: CLPL-2280
Title: "CASSETTE"
Length: 30 SECONDS

"Do do de dum. . ."

CUSTOMER: Madge, I really <u>dig</u> rock!

MADGE: These hands <u>look</u> like you've been digging rock.

CUSTOMER: It's dishwashing. What'll I try?

MADGE: Everything. . .and use Palmolive Liquid.

You're softening in it.

CUSTOMER: Mmm. . .feels soft, like a lotion. Must be mild.

But how does it clean?

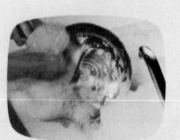

MADGE: Great!
ANNCR: Right, Madge. Palmolive cleans away the toughest grease.

Leaves dishes and pans spotless!

MADGE: And Palmolive softens hands while you do dishes.

(TWO WEEKS LATER)
CUSTOMER: Madge, Palmolive is really cool!

MADGE: I thought it was <u>chilly</u> in here!

Remember, Palmolive softens hands while you do dishes.

so natural, only her hairdresser knows for sure."

At first broadcasters and magazine editors were leery of the sexual innuendo they perceived in the line "Does she or doesn't she?" Surveys showed this to be a male bias only, and so the ads were run. They used natural women as models instead of the glamour-girl types who were in vogue during the fifties. American women empathised with this approach. Only 7 percent of them had ever dyed their hair prior to Polykoff's campaign. After the siege, the number rose to 50 percent.

"Ads that communicate and really create a compelling person-to-person bond are ads that reflect the writer's total life experience," says Polykoff. In 1964, she again faced the task of in-

troducing a new product, Nice 'n' Easy Shampoo-In Hair Color. "My mind wandered back to those early days when my husband, George, and I used to meet each other after work. I'd first glimpse him coming down the block, and we'd fly toward each other. But compared to our eagerness to bridge the distance, it was like wading through molasses. He'd lift me off my feet and say, 'You know, you look pretty good from afar.' 'And from near?' I'd ask. 'Even better.' " From that memory, Polykoff created a commercial that showed a young couple running toward each other through a field, in slow motion, while the announcer intoned, "The closer you get . . . the better you look."

"Is it true blondes have more fun?" Clairol did as much to popularize blondes as did the state of California. (Foote, Cone & Belding, 1965)

Another of Polykoff's famous "arresting question" slogans was, "Is it true blondes have more fun?" Although the jingle was never released as a record in the United States, "Is It True?" became a hit song in the Soviet Union in October 1965. "It's too bad Clairol had no product distribution in the U.S.S.R. . . . ," Polykoff jokes. "We might have changed the whole political complexion of the country from red to blond!"

For Miss Loving Care, Polykoff asked viewers, "Hate that gray? Wash it away!" She even employed existential philosophy in the Clairol campaign of the sixties, challenging reincarnation beliefs with her bold declaration, "If I have but one life to live, let me live it as a blonde!"

COMING A LONG WAY

Virginia Slims' slogan, "You've come a long way, baby," became closely identified with the burgeoning women's liberation movement of the late sixties and early seventies. Philip Morris, the New York-based cigarette conglomerate, and its agency, Leo Burnett, both claim they did not intend any political overtones to the campaign. But the Virginia Slims ads, like all heavily promoted commercials, were seen with such frequency that they, the first TV ads to acknowledge the change in women's roles in American culture, were viewed as lighthearted feminist vignettes.

All the "plots" were similar. A Victorian-era woman is forced to sneak a puff from a cigarette because the reigning patriarchy disapproves of ladies smoking. In one ad, a husband discovers his wife smoking a cigarette in the basement behind the preserves. He spanks her. Another woman brazenly smokes on a public beach, wearing a one-piece bathing suit, no less, and is promptly arrested. "And then, in 1920," says the announcer as a suffragette parade marches by, "women won their rights." A drum roll brings us up to the present, where the woman of 1970 models the latest fashions against a bright white backdrop. A male chorus sings the celebratory jingle: "You've come a long way, baby. . ."

Virginia Slims soon became the leading women's cigarette. Some of the top fashion de-signers whose outfits were featured in the series included Halston, Calvin Klein, Christian Dior, Ralph Lauren, Adolpho, and Bill Blass. Although cigarette ads disappeared from TV on January 2, 1971, Virginia Slims' magazine ads carry on the campaign today. Based on the old television commercials, they juxtapose sepia-toned photos of turn-of-the-century drudges with the chic women of the eighties modeling the latest designs. The ads say women have indeed come a long way, although the critical viewer of 1984 might consider a woman executive to be a more suitable representative of the gender's progress than a dressed-up model.

The first true "women's lib" ad, however, one that liberated its protagonist from the traditional role of housewife and sensitively portrayed her real-life problems, came from an unexpected sponsor—Hallmark. The Kansas City-based greeting card company's 1971 commercial, "What a Day!" was in many ways revolutionary. It showed a woman as an empathetic, unglamorous, vulnerable human being. The film was directed by Walt Topel, whos ability to elicit understated, sensitive performances from his actors has made classics out of Dial's "First Date" commercial and Kimbies diapers' "First Time Father." Jim Drain of Hallmark's agency, Foote, Cone & Belding, wrote the script, which tells the story of a young single working woman on a particularly difficult day.

Racing to work one morning, the woman spots her cat in the hallway. She does an about-face to let the cat back into her apartment, forgetting her umbrella on the stair railing. She then misses the bus by seconds, arrives late for work, and receives a reproachful glance from her supervisor. She completes a stack of files, only to have a sheepish office boy deposit an even larger stack on her desk an instant later. At lunch, she sits silently as a co-worker hogs the conversation. The office is dark and empty when the woman finally finishes her work. The bus lets her off in the midst of a rainstorm, and as she trudges back up the stairs to her apartment, she retrieves her abandoned umbrella with quiet resignation.

At this point, viewers are wondering what the payoff will be. Is this long, two-minute ad for an antidepressant? A suicide-prevention hot line? But no, the commercial is too honest for

such a melodramatic ending. The young woman, soaked and exausted, enters her apartment and sifts through the mail. One envelope attracts her attention and she opens it. Inside is a greeting card. As she reads the message, the woman smiles. The announcer says, "Hallmark. When you care enough to send the very best."

The original script for "What a Day!" was filled with dialogue, but director Topel wisely threw it all out. As a result, few silent films since Chaplin have combined humor and pathos so well. And as a statement to both women and men about the trials and loneliness of the big-city working world, no other commercial has matched the social realism of Hallmark's little drama.

EMANCIPATION

The seemingly impossible task of chronicling, in a mere thirty seconds, the liberated "new" woman, involved in her triple role as wife, mother, and working woman, was stylishly accomplished in 1978 in the Enjoli perfume commercial "24 Hour Woman." Loraine Bauchmann, marketing director for Charles of the Ritz, Enjoli's manufacturer, says, "We are celebrating the growth of women. To be, to do, and

to cope; we are showing all a woman has taken on in life."

Pam Huntington, a California model, was cast by Advertising to Women, the agency that created the Enjoli ad, to star in the commercial. According to Bauchmann, "She's very feminine, very sure of herself, very confident, and doesn't take everything too seriously, which was important because we never claimed the '24 Hour Woman' was perfection. We see her as being very human."

On the commercial's soundtrack, a female jazz vocalist performs Peggy Lee's "I'm a Woman" as Huntington pantomimes her day's activities, appearing first in a business suit, flaunting a wad of bills ("I can bring home the bacon . . ."), then, in slacks and a loose shirt to tackle kitchen chores (" . . . fry it up in a pan . . ."), and finally in a low-slung, champagne-hued gown, beautifully made up (" . . . and never let you forget you're a man!"). As she sits down to read bedtime stories to her unseen children, a man's offscreen voice says affectionately, "Tonight, I'm gonna cook for the kids!"—a further acknowledgment of changing sex roles, done also with a light touch that was nonthreatening to the male viewer.

The popularity of the emancipated "24 Hour Woman" helped make Enjoli the third-best-selling fragrance in the United States in

NEW TV COMMERCIAL-MOST EXCITING EVER
ENJOLI "The 24 hour woman II" LENGTH: 30 SECONDS

LYRICS FEMALE SINGER:
'Cause

I'm a woman -

Enjoli!

I can bring home the bacon. Enjoli!

Fry it up in a pan -

Enjoli!

And never let you forget you're a man.

VO: GIVE HER ENJOLI! THE 8 HOUR PERFUME

FOR THE 24 HOUR WOMAN.

LYRICS FEMALE SINGER:
I can work till 5 o'clock!

Come home and read you tickety tock.

MALE SINGER: (VO) Tonight I'm gonna cook for the kids!

LYRICS FEMALE SINGER:
And if it's lovin' you want

I can kiss you and give ya the shiverin' fits!

VO: ENJOLI THE 8 HOUR PERFUME

FOR YOUR 24 HOUR WOMAN

PRETESTED BY INDEPENDENT RESEARCH STUDY
CHARLES OF THE RITZ GROUP LTD. © CHARLES OF THE RITZ GROUP LTD. 1980

1978. Of the top five perfumes, Enjoli was the only one to enjoy a "growth pattern," or an increase in sales every year through 1982. Of course, the introductory commercial brought in the buyers, but, as Richard Loniewsky, the perfumer at Charles of the Ritz who creates new fragrances, points out, "Without the juice, you can forget it." The same can be said for any product—its quality must hold up in the marketplace, no matter how interesting its commercials.

The timeliness of the Enjoli ad was helped by a "focus group." This particular focus group consisted of a selection of female consumers called together by the Advertising to Women agency to discuss their concerns and hopes. It was this "qualitative market research" that led to the creation of the "24 Hour Woman," embodying as she does the aspirations of so many contemporary women.

The commercials for Revlon's perfume Charlie also managed to capture the female *Zeitgeist* of the seventies and eighties. In 1976, singer Bobby Short sat at a nightclub piano and sang, "There's a fragrance that's here today, and they call it Charlie . . ." In swept model Shelley Hack on the wings of emancipation and male adoration. Hack personified Revlon's Charlie the way Tom Selleck later personified Revlon's Chaz, and, like Selleck, she became a role model of the late seventies. The job description for the female lead in the commercial entitled "New York" read as follows: "Charlie must be able to walk down the street smoothly. She's outgoing, purposeful. She knows where she's going, and she's not dependent on any man." Hack was able to bring to the role of this independent woman a vibrant beauty that contrasted noticeably with the unglamorous feminists of the time.

"New York" also made a national celebrity of Bobby Short, the saloon singer, or "song stylist," at Manhattan's Carlyle Hotel, the favored hangout for the group at Revlon's in-house ad agency, the Fiftieth Floor Workshop (which is located, oddly enough, on the forty-sixth floor of the General Motors Building). Short appears in the commercial singing the Charlie jingle as Shelley Hack makes her rousing nightclub entrance. In a similar commercial filmed one year later and entitled "Afloat," crooner Mel Torme sang at the piano of a barge floating down the Seine in Paris, entertaining Hack and her new commercial boyfriend. Torme would later include the Charlie jingle in his own nightclub act.

Feminine ideals change. Charlie's recent commercial, "After the Party," was Revlon's way of saying "We're getting more sophisticated"; the new Charlie Girl was Tamara Norman, described as "the warmer, softer, mellower woman of 1983." In "After the Party," Norman and her man wander the midnight streets of New York, their love safeguarding them from Gotham's nighttime perils. As dawn breaks and a romantic rendition of the Charlie theme plays, the peripatetic couple discuss marriage in a flip, breezy manner until—surprise!—Charlie says she likes the idea. The timeless proposal seems fresh and glamorous, just as the return to romanticism becomes the latest word in feminine fulfillment. TV commercials mirror the swing of the consumer society's social pendulum.

No sociological study has yet been made that correlates the attitudes of contemporary American society toward sexual roles with the images depicted in the commercials of the time. Much might be learned, for instance, from Geritol's notorious commercials of the early seventies. When these were first aired, nascent feminist sensibilities had yet to find a voice sufficient to criticize the husbands in the commercials who, after complimenting their wives on taking care of the kids, keeping house, etc., confide to the viewer, "I think I'll keep her." Feminists, who felt that the husbands considered their spouses little more than chattels, by mid-decade had made their fury known to J. B. Williams, Geritol's manufacturer. Since that time, the husbands' closing remarks after touting their wives' accomplishments, including liberal imbibing of the sponsor's product, have concluded with, "And I love her for it." This example serves to illustrate how closely commercials are allied to the society they serve. Geritol's ads were restructured because of changes in roles and womens' relationships with men. The behind-the-scenes social forces that come to bear on advertising always influence how a sponsor sells its product. The television commercial is indeed a time capsule. It's a glamorized record of our evolving consumer society.

REVLON

Charlie

1978

"AFLOAT"　　　　　　　　　　　　:30 COLOR　　　　　　　　　　　　RVCH1643

SINGER: There's a fragrance

that's here today...

and they call it

Charlie.

A different fragrance

that thinks your way.

Yeah, they call it Charlie.

Kinda young. Kinda now. Charlie.

Kinda free. Kinda wow. Charlie.

Kinda fragrance that's gonna stay. And
it's here now.

Charlie.

ANNCR: (VO) Now the world belongs to
Charlie, by Revlon.

FIFTIETH FLOOR WORKSHOP, 1978

REVLON
Charlie

"AFTER THE PARTY" :30

RVCF 1143

(MUSIC UNDER)
HE: Nice party.

ANNCR: (VO) The best part of the party's when the party's over.

HE: Mmm, Charlie?
SHE: Uh huh.

HE: Would you cancel your trip to the coast if I proposed?

SHE: I wonder how much this lion weighs?

HE: Ciao!
SHE: Great bakery!

HE: Listen, I'm serious about what I said before.
SHE: Eat your breakfast.

HE: Even my mother thinks it's time for you to settle down.

SHE: Your mother's right.

ANNCR: (VO) Charlie. It's a great life.

Chapter Three

Men in Commercials

"Here's Good

Male role models in commercials have not changed as dramatically as have female role models during the last thirty-five years, yet men have also experienced a form of "liberation." They have not suffered from social and economic inequities, but rather from a limiting emotional stoicism. This has led to the recent "new sensitivity" of men,

to Friends!"

which is now reflected in commercials. Thirty years ago, the father lorded it over his family as the wise, responsible breadwinner, compassionate but not intimate. Today the commercial father will be more emotionally open. He will also defer to his wife, act the buffoon with his children, do housework, and admit mistakes. This is a radical change

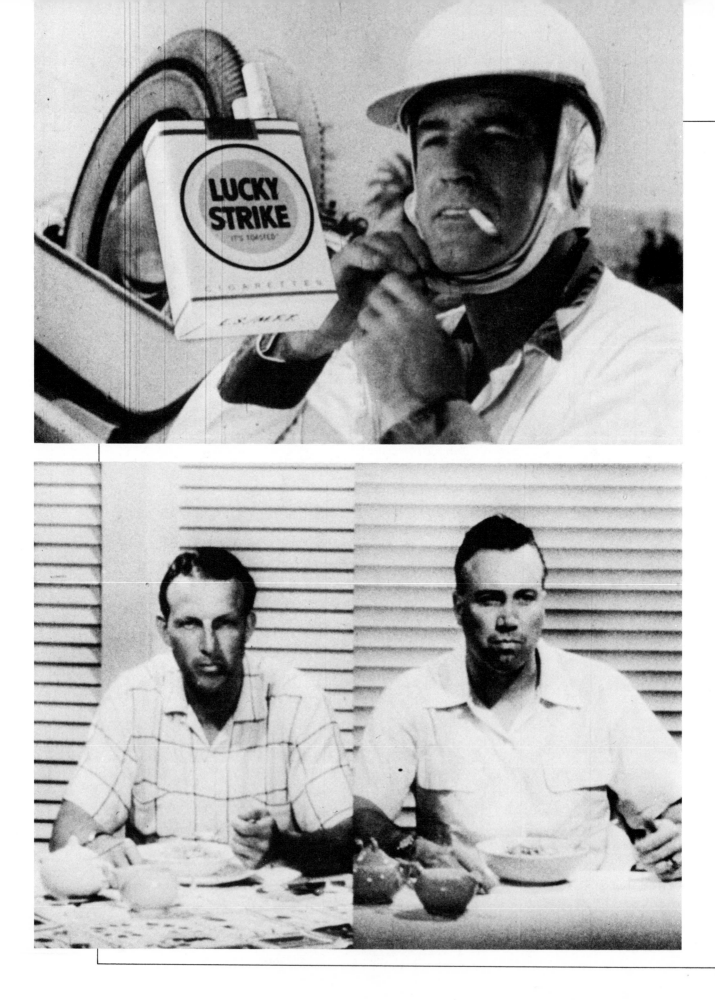

Having wrecked a car, a movie stunt-man enjoys a Lucky Strike as he poses beside his shattered vehicle. Though not always as violently expressed as in this effort from the fifties, machismo is the prevailing element in so-called men's commercials. (Laurence, Charles & Free, circa 1955)

Duke Snider and Stan "the Man" Musial of the Brooklyn Dodgers start their day with Wheaties, "The Breakfast of Champions." More than any other sponsor, Wheaties has traditionally employed jocks as its spokesmen. These "idols of youth" are enshrined as popular male role models. (Fitzgerald Advertising, 1953)

John Cameron Swayze tapes a Timex to the bow of a speedboat. Swayze was a respected newscaster during the early years of television, and when Timex signed him, it had a spokesman with a ready-made reputation for credibility. His "torture test" commercials ran for twenty years. (Grey Advertising, 1968)

from the days when any critical portrayal of the head of the household would be thought to undermine the American family, thus weakening the foundation of the country.

Since TV commercials reflect our society, one might gather from viewing the ads of the fifties that the country was less emotionally sanguine during that decade. Men were he-men in the commercials of thirty years ago. They were well-groomed, unemotional, and happiest away from home enjoying the company of other men. "Welcome to a *man's* world," intoned an announcer as we were ushered into the sanctum sanctorum of "The Men's Club," a Raleigh pipe tobacco ad. A quartet in flannel shirts and hunting boots pose before a stone-faced fireplace, admiring the head of a moose someone has shot. It is a tableau of masculinity. But along with this masculinity came an unnaturalness; during the fifties, men were constantly "posing" in commercials. In Lucky Strike's commercials, a man practiced target shooting

with a machine gun (how could he miss?), another man wrecked a stunt car, and both stood smoking and admiring their damage with self-satisfied grins.

Perhaps because these male role models tried to embody too much—the postwar patriarch's intensity of purpose in both work and play, a man trying to reconcile corporate conformity with rugged individualism—commercial men of the fifties were as lifeless as mannequins. The celebrities of the fifties were certainly more colorful than today's TV-wise superstars. Yet in TV commercials, they appeared stodgy and dull. In Wheaties' ads, for example, Brooklyn Dodgers' sluggers Duke Snider and Stan "the Man" Musial sat before bowls of cereal and simply glowered at the camera. The message in these ads was clear: Real men express themselves through direct action, like hitting homers or wrecking stunt cars. In repose they are taciturn and—unless they were in the company of other men—inexpressive.

SPOKESMEN: THE FIRST GENERATION

The principal role of men in commercials continues to be, as it was from the beginning, that of the "spokesman." The approach may be authoritative or intimate, but these men project a credibility that makes viewers trust them. Spokesmen tell us to "do as I say." It is the degree of skill and subtlety with which this command is given that determines the truly effective spokesman.

For twenty years, a former TV newscaster, John Cameron Swayze, hosted a variety of "torture tests" designed to prove the invincibility of Timex watches. The "demonstration commercial" has been a popular commercial staple over the years, bringing us an elephant stepping on an uncrushable Tonka toy, a gorilla brutalizing a piece of Samsonite luggage, and a stuntman driving a Fiat over a waterfall. Thanks to Swayze's deadpan credibility, the Timex commercials proved the most enduring. Swayze was the host of NBC's *Camel News Caravan* in 1952, when the watch manufacturer asked him to do a series of "live" tests. The audience watched, fascinated, as he tossed a Timex into a paint mixer. A few clattering seconds later, Swayze held up the battered watch and presented his verdict, an oft-repeated piece of advertising doggerel: "It takes a licking, but it keeps on ticking!"

Not all the live demonstration commercials ended so well. On the *Steve Allen Show*, Swayze strapped a Timex to an outboard motor, and after the propeller stopped spinning, the watch was nowhere to be found. Swayze sloshed around the tank, assuring viewers that "it worked perfectly during rehearsals," while Allen laughed hysterically off camera.

Swayze taped watches to the ankle of a professional water skier, to the wrist of a high diver, to the leg of a racehorse, to the bow of a speedboat, and abused the timepieces in more than forty other offbeat situations until his retirement in 1972. To keep the ads honest, engineers always inspected the watches after they had been "tortured." Swayze became so closely identified with his commercials that "strangers on the street would walk up to me and pull up my sleeve to see if I was wearing a Timex. Of course, I wear one religiously."

Ed Reimers stands amid the devastation of Hurricane Carla, in 1962. Here, footage of the Texas tragedy is recorded on videotape, just then coming into use. (Leo Burnett, 1962)

For three decades, one of the most familiar spokesmen of all time was actor Ed Reimers. He appeared almost magically in the wake of disaster. Calmly offering solace to victims whose homes had been destroyed, Reimers would assure them, "You're in good hands with Allstate." These startling, documentary-style commercials remained so forceful that each new episode appeared to be as fresh as the first, which was aired on the *Playhouse 90* program in 1957.

Allstate was the first insurance company to use television advertising extensively. The Leo Burnett agency cast Reimers in the spokesman's role because the authority and credibility

he radiated evoked the sense of security that people desired from an insurance representative. "You're in good hands with Allstate" became, in the words of a company ad manager, "the best-recognized slogan in the casualty insurance business—the whole philosophy of the company in one quick line."

Whenever disaster struck, dozens of Allstate claims adjusters rushed to the scene to settle claims, often arriving ahead of rival insurance companies. To dramatize this quick action, camera crews were dispatched to those front-page disaster areas to produce commercials. These ads were on the air within days, while the tragedy was still newsworthy. Reimers would interview victims amid the rubble of their shattered homes, a ghoulish business until the policyholders informed us that their properties would soon be replaced, thanks to the alacrity of the Allstate claims representatives.

New technologies were often employed to get the ads on the air swiftly. The devastation of Hurricane Carla in 1962 was the basis for one of the first commercials recorded on videotape. And Ed Reimers's trip to the tornado-ravaged town of Xenia, Ohio, in 1974 was seen by viewers only three days after he stood surrounded by rubble and cupped his hands together in the famous "good hands" gesture, symbolizing security amid the mayhem.

The Marlboro Man lights up. (Leo Burnett, 1969)

SPOKESMEN OF LEGENDS AND FARCE

When one considers the prominence of the cowboy in American culture, it comes as a surprise that only Marlboro has employed the cowboy as an identifiable character over an extended period of time. The Marlboro Man was created in the mid-sixties, and he can still be seen in magazines and on billboards. He also continues to ride the range on overseas television, where cigarette advertising has not been banned from the air, and where he has come to personify the modern American West.

Philip Morris, Marlboro's manufacturer, introduced the brand in the early fifties as a woman's cigarette. When this strategy failed, Marlboro inaugurated a new approach, touting the brand as the most masculine cigarette on the market. The original Marlboro Men were rugged outdoorsmen—campers, canoeists, hunters. But in the sixties, *the* Marlboro Man, the familiar cowboy, another identifiable-character creation of the Leo Burnett agency, rode into video folklore.

The Marlboro Man was played by a succession of actors and actual cowboys over the years. The invitation "Come to Where the Flavor Is" is followed in each commercial by scenes of the Marlboro Man riding horseback over the plains, rounding up cattle, or relaxing beside the campfire in the mountain snow. Here, then, is a *real*, as opposed to a contrived, man's world, or so the ads propose—a world both idyllic and legendary. Rarely has a product evoked such memorable imagery.

The rugged Marlboro Man made his brand of cigarettes the top seller in the world. Smokers were clearly purchasing an image with each pack, but it was a multilayered image. In what was perhaps his best commercial, "Wild Stallions," the Marlboro Man calls off his ranch hands, who are about to catch a wild horse that has been chasing away their best mares. As the Marlboro Man watches the beautiful beast gallop away, expressions of respect and wistful admiration play over his face, proving there is more to this cowboy than the macho stereotype.

Mindless machismo, however, proved to be a target of potent satire in Vicks Formula 44 cough syrup ads of the late sixties. One of the movies' great heavies, Harold Sakata, best known for his portrayal of Oddjob in the James Bond thriller *Goldfinger*, starred in a series of violent, slapstick farces. The scenario was the same for each ad: Sakata, irritated by a throat tickle, would systematically karate-chop his surroundings to rubble until his wife fed him a spoonful of Vicks. He tore through an art gallery in one commercial, decapitating priceless statues, and in his most spectacular spree, he took apart a suburban neighborhood. Whenever a guttural cough would explode from his throat, Sakata's deadly hand would reflexively shoot out and chop anything in his way. "Harold was actually a very gentle man," recalls director John Urie. "He really enjoyed his Oddjob character, and had a lot of fun with it."

So did viewers. In his last commercial, Sakata is stuffed inside a crowded elevator. He coughs. Like his panic-stricken wife, viewers anticipate chaos. In the end, though, the strong man smiles benignly at his fellow passengers, whose lives have been spared by a cough drop.

PATERFAMILIAS

Even the most casual viewer cannot help noticing that commercial spokeswomen are invariably attractive and young, although lack of good looks has never inhibited the credibility of spokesmen and age has often polished the patina of their authority. Certainly the least likely to become the patriarch of all male commercial pitchmen during the sixties and seventies was Colonel Harland Sanders.

Colonel Sanders became one of the world's most familiar faces as an identifiable character for the Louisville-based Kentucky Fried Chicken chain that he had founded in the 1950s. Sanders opened his first restaurant in Corbin, Kentucky, in 1932. Sanders' Court and Cafe was a combination restaurant, service station, and motel. He appeared in dozens of commercials from 1964 until his death at the age of ninety in 1980. The Colonel was seen attired in his white suit, string tie, and snow-white goatee and mustache at picnics, barbecues, and other down-home occasions where his "finger-lickin' good" chicken, prepared with its "secret blend of eleven herbs and spices" was served.

The Kentucky Fried Chicken Company initially had no television advertising budget, and it was entirely on the basis of the Colonel's personality and skill as a homespun storyteller on TV talk shows and programs, such as *What's My Line?*, that the franchise garnered a reputation. When Sanders finally appeared in commercials, his scripts placed him in bizarre situations—one ad from the mid-sixties had angry housewives kidnap the Colonel, tie him up in an abandoned warehouse, and demand that he reveal his secret recipe.

Harold Sakata, wearing the costume of Oddjob, practices a karate chop in this rehearsal for a Vicks Formula 44 cough syrup commercial. (Benton & Bowles, 1968)

As the cameras roll, Oddjob demolishes a museum piece. (Benton & Bowles, 1968)

Sanders's commercial persona crystallized in the ads created by the Leo Burnett agency. "His best were the ones that involved kids," recalls a longtime Sanders associate, John Cox, now a public relations executive with the R. J. Reynolds Industries Food and Beverage Group, the conglomerate that acquired Kentucky Fried Chicken. "The Colonel had tremendous affection for kids, and they would feel it. To them, he was a combination grandfather and Santa Claus. They'd love to sit on his lap. We'd be shooting a commercial and it would be a schoolday, but all of a sudden dozens of kids would come running up to him. We never could find out what radar they used to track down the Colonel." It was this playful empathy between Sanders and children that stamped him as commercials' genial grandfather.

Fictional fathers in video ads have often appeared stilted and contrived when they have tried to express the conflicting attitudes of authority and affection toward their make-believe families. It is a difficult role, almost as difficult as being a real-life father. One of commercials' most believable papas was a real one—Bing Crosby. He appeared with his wife Kathryn and their three youngest children in ads for Minute Maid orange juice. Crosby helped establish the frozen orange juice business by promoting the first concentrate, "as good as fresh-squeezed," at a time when only awful-tasting canned orange juices were the conventional substitute for fresh. Everyone who listened to Bing croon about Minute Maid on his radio show, and later, on his daytime TV show of the fifties, was convinced he owned the company. Minute Maid's founder, the legendary John "Jock" Whitney, did induce Crosby to invest in the company, and then awarded him a West Coast distributorship, which he owned until 1958. Ten years later, the Marschalk Company, the ad agency for Minute Maid (now a subsidiary of Coca-Cola), tried to lure Crosby back into commercials for its new "The Best There

Is" campaign. Bing was reluctant. He finally agreed to be the voice-over announcer if his children could appear in the ads, giving them their acting debuts. (Today, Harry Crosby, Jr., has chosen to make acting his profession, and daughter Mary Frances became Christen, the woman who shot J.R. on *Dallas*, while Nathaniel won the 1981 Amateur Golf Championship, pursuing another of his father's passions.)

Minute Maid produced one commercial a year showing the Crosby family making orange juice in their Hillsboro, California, home or aboard their boat moored in San Francisco Bay. In the fourth year, 1972, Crosby made a cameo appearance when he drove onto the set in his customized golf cart. He took over after that, appearing without his family until his death in 1977. The following year, Kathryn

Crosby and the kids, who had grown up in the commercials, made one final installment, with Bing seen in a portrait.

The Marschalk Company was originally concerned that the rebellious youth of the late sixties and early seventies would be turned off by Crosby as paterfamilias at a time when such institutions as the family were being questioned. But surveys showed that youthful viewers responded favorably to the superstar of their parents' generation, perhaps because the family scenes in the Minute Maid ads were so relaxed and appealing. Despite later claims by Crosby's children from an earlier marriage that their father was tyrannical, the playfulness he displayed in the "Best There Is" ads made the "imitation" fathers of other commercials seem lifeless by comparison.

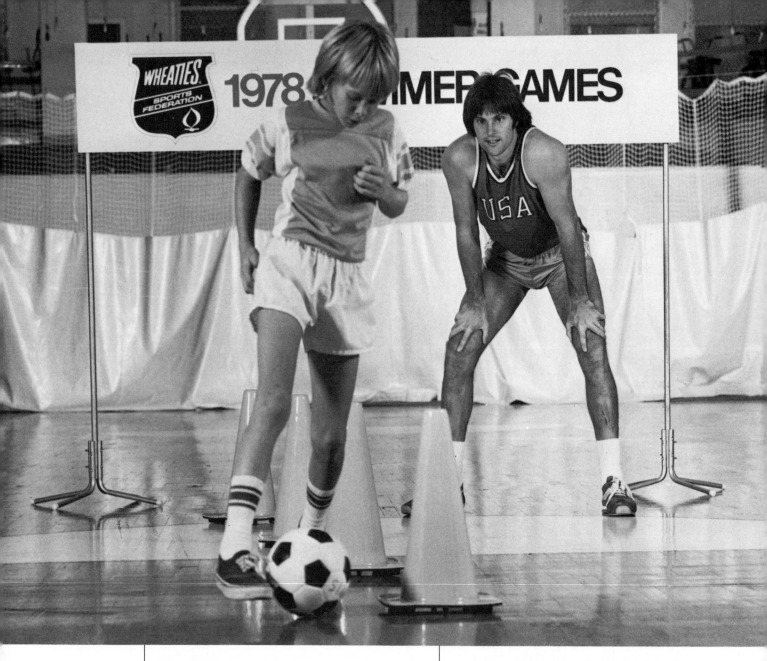

SPOKESMEN AS ROLE MODELS

The burning question asked by all little boys—
what type of man do I want to grow up to be,
and how do I do it?—has been consistently addressed over the years by at least one sponsor—
Wheaties. "The Breakfast of Champions" has
been associated with the "idols of youth,"
whom boys emulated on the sandlot and play-
ground ever since the cereal signed up Babe
Ruth as an endorser in the early thirties. The
fifties saw a series of regional commercials for
children's television that used local heroes like
baseball stars Ted Williams and Mickey Mantle
to inspire boys to eat Wheaties and grow up to
be champs. General Mills has had an unerring
eye for choosing celebrity jocks that appeal to
youngsters. Boyish Bruce Jenner was signed in

1977 after winning the decathlon gold medal in
the Montreal Olympics. In his commercial,
documentary footage showed Jenner at the decathlon finish line, where he was handed a
small American flag and suddenly became a
contemporary version of Wheaties' earliest
hero, Jack Armstrong, "the all-American boy."
Viewers next saw Jenner at the breakfast table,
testifying that he has been eating the cereal all
his life.

In a case of consumer protectionism run
rampant, the assistant district attorney in San
Francisco brought suit against General Mills.
The charge: consumer fraud. The claim: Jenner
didn't *really* eat Wheaties. The press had a field
day. Jenner called a news conference and announced, "I don't like people thinking I am not
telling the truth. Wheaties has been in my diet

Wheaties continued its "idols of youth" series in 1977, when it featured boyish Bruce Jenner, the decathlon champ of the 1976 Olympic Games. (Dancer Fitzgerald Sample, 1978)

for years." As proof, he challenged the DA to ask his mother. The suit was dropped—and so, in time, was Jenner, when he proved to have negligible effect on sales, although he was retained by the Wheaties Sports Federation for its annual Children's Olympics.

Bill Cosby is also thought by many to be a laudable role model. Since the seventies, Cosby has pitched such diverse products as Apple computers and Jell-O brand gelatin and pudding. Among his contemporaries as black spokespeople are Ella Fitzgerald for Memorex recording tape, Arthur Ashe for Head tennis rackets, O. J. Simpson for Hertz, and other entertainment and sports figures. Among Hispanic spokesmen, however, Ricardo Montalban stands alone.

Ricardo Montalban poses beside a Chrysler Cordoba. The first Hispanic spokesman, Montalban, for years a successful film actor, is considered a role model for Mexican Americans. (Kenyon & Eckhardt, 1978)

Frank Sinatra, *center,* is given a tour of Chrysler's Detroit automotive plant by Lee Iacocca, *left.* (Kenyon & Eckhardt, 1979)

A 1983 *Los Angeles Times* survey among Southern California's sizable Hispanic community found Montalban second only to the United Farm Workers' founder Cesar Chavez as the most admired Mexican American. He had been highly visible for ten years when, in 1973, the elegant, gentlemanly actor began his reign as pitchman for the Chrysler Cordoba.

The commercials of Chrysler have also been the source of an unlikely but nonetheless influential role model: the successful big businessman. At a time when corporate chieftains were never seen in TV ads, Lee Iacocca cheerled his way through a campaign that helped salvage a company that teetered on the edge of bankruptcy in 1979-80.

Chairman Iacocca, the former Ford *Wunderkind* and father of the Mustang, was pounding the table at a creative meeting with Chrysler's agency, Kenyon & Eckhardt, insisting, "We've got the best automotive technology in the world. Dammit, the Japanese steal from *us*!" Iacocca's words were transcribed into script form, and he was asked to record them for a commercial that took viewers inside the company's massive automotive plant in Detroit. Chrysler was perceived as an underdog at the time, and viewers were treated to the spectacle of Iacocca, feisty and determined, defending his

product and challenging his listeners: "If you can find a better car, buy it!"

The chairman was soon swamped with a four-foot-high daily stack of mail from viewers who wished him well. They wrote to say they believed his message. Iacocca's reply was the same to all his fans: "Buy a car!"

One admirer called Iacocca directly. "Lee," he said, "this is Frank Sinatra. I like what you're doing on TV. You've got guts. I want you to know if there's anything I can do..." Savvily, the Chrysler chairman of the board invited the "Chairman of the Board" up to Detroit to inspect his plant. The visit was recorded on film and became the basis for the first of the Sinatra-Iacocca television commercials. Auto buyers seemed as convinced as Sinatra, and within a year, Chrysler was creeping back from the brink.

THE "EXPERT" SPOKESMEN

If an actor can project sincere authority and stalwart credibility, he will be accepted as a moral force worthy of trust for the message he conveys. Beginning in the early seventies, Americans took their automotive advice not from a mechanic, but from a bespectacled actor named Ben Hayes, who looked like a techni-

Ben Hayes, Shell Oil's "Answer Man," was an "expert" spokesman whose specialty was automotive problems. (Ogilvy & Mather, 1976)

cian. Hayes was the "Shell Answer Man," and as his moniker implies, he knew all about cars. His most elaborate ad was a torture test more sophisticated than anyting John Cameron Swayze might have dreamt of. Shell's agency, Ogilvy & Mather, produced "Fire and Ice" in 1976; in the ad, an automobile is subjected to the ancient Roman gladiatoral rite, the "ordeal of fire and water," to demonstrate the temperature tolerance of Shell's motor oil. The car's engine was lubricated with the oil before the entire car was frozen in a block of ice. After thawing, the same car was forced to pull a 60,000-pound crane over the Mojave Desert. The oil neither froze nor boiled.

To produce the ad, a special six-sided freezer was constructed around the car. The laborious process of encasing the vehicle in a photogenic block of ice had to be repeated because a compressor broke down during the initial attempt. Finally, after a week, Ben Hayes was photographed crawling through a tunnel that had been hacked into the automotive ice cube. The ignition kicked over at his touch, and Hayes flashed the "thumbs up" sign. The next day was spent unthawing the car, using jackhammers to break up the ice. Then the stalwart sedan, a Ford, was hitched to a construction crane and driven through the sagebrush and white sands of the Mojave. The engine temperature exceeded 270 degrees, but the oil held. A quarter of a million dollars and six months of production time were spent on the thirty-second ad. The sales of Shell Fire and Ice motor oil, according to a Shell spokesman, increased "spectacularly."

Often, an actor whose area of expertise is well known to the public is enlisted to play himself in a commercial, to endorse a product on the basis of his taste. One of the delights of late-seventies television was the sight of an imposing, bearded Orson Welles sitting before a glass of burgundy and rumbling, "At Paul Masson, we will sell no wine before its time." Welles, a recognized connoisseur, did for his California sponsor what Bing Crosby had done for Minute Maid: he firmly established the brand in the viewers' minds. Paul Masson's sales went from a distant fourth behind Inglenook, Almaden, and Gallo, up to a tie for the first place with Gallo Brothers.

Welles was just one of several stars, including Gregory Peck and Charlton Heston, first considered by the Doyle Dane Bernbach agency to act as spokesman for Masson's "Time and Care" campaign. These commercials, emphasizing the patience and skill required to produce quality wine, would be the first national commercials for the brand. Winemaking had once been a "gentlemen's profession" among the family-owned wineries of Central California's Napa and Sonoma valleys. That changed by the seventies, when wine consumption in the United States skyrocketed, and the conglomerates moved in to take over the business.

Seagram's acquired Paul Masson and was prepared to promote its varietals with a substantial advertising budget. Consumers were quizzed on possible spokesmen, and Welles was favored. The style and elegance he lent to Paul Masson's wines helped the sponsor, at least psychologically, to justify the somewhat higher price of its product.

Beginning in 1979, Welles was seen in a variety of situations—promoting Chablis at the Masson winery in Saratoga, California, speaking about champagne at a formal party, pouring burgundy at a barbecue, enjoying Rhine Castle wine at a German castle garden recreated in Hollywood. In 1980, he began to compare the "winemaker's art" with the dedication and genius responsible for Beethoven's symphonies and Margaret Mitchell's *Gone With the Wind*. By this time, viewers were so familiar with one of commercials' most famous slogans, that they would shout back to their television sets, accompanying Welles's sonorous baritone: "We will sell no wine before its time." The "wear-out factor" was the reason for Welles's retirement in 1982.

Another prestigious actor, Robert Morley, is credited with much of the success of British Airways in the United States. Before Morley first appeared on TV in 1971, BOAC, as the carrier was then known, was perceived by consumers as stuffy and cold. It was assigned all the negative characteristics Americans commonly attribute to the British. But with his buoyant girth and jovial manner, the effusive Morley reminded viewers that there was another side to the British character. Suddenly it was considered "fun" to fly British Air from "the Colonies" to the landmarks of England, which were highlighted in the ads with Morley acting as tour guide.

British expatriates in America wrote angry letters to the Campbell-Ewald agency, which hed created the campaign, complaining that the comedic Robert Morley was not truly representative of Englishmen. But the popularity of the ads grew, and the critics became fond of Morley because his conviviality was not faked. Off camera, Morley takes a proprietary interest in "his" airline. Passengers approach him during flights aboard British Air and thank him for a smooth trip; they also hold him responsible if delays occur. During one particularly lengthy delay, Morley was nearly overrun by derisive passengers. He retreated into the cockpit and asked the captain to serve a free round of drinks "on the house." The captain agreed. The announcement was made over the loudspeaker, and an ovation greeted Morley when he reappeared in the cabin. It is not uncommon for an actor to be so closely identified with one of his characters that his public and private personas merge, as is the case with Robert Morley, the jolly Englishman of the skies.

NEW IMAGES

By the late seventies, partially as a result of the women's liberation movement, which prompted a reappraisal of all sexual roles, men in commercials had begun to shed their tough-guy demeanors. Joe Namath radically aided this trend when he donned a pair of pantyhose for Hanes. In 1980, welterweight champion Sugar Ray Leonard was portrayed not as the traditional killer of the ring, but, "Feeling Seven-Up," he was shown trading affectionate mock punches with his five-year-old son. TV commercials, once again acting as social barometers, recorded the winds of change that were freeing men to be more open and tolerant. The traditional father figure could even risk looking foolish, a liberty no commercial-maker would have dared to take in the fifties.

"Role reversal" ads were coming into vogue around this time. These commercials asked: If women can conquer fields once considered male domains, why can't men do the reverse?

Englishman Robert Morley points the way for British Airways. Here, too, an "expert" spokesman had a tremendous positive effect on the sponsor's sales. (Campbell- Ewald, 1976)

THE QUAKER OATS COMPANY

AUNT JEMIMA FRENCH TOAST
"FATHER & SON RAISIN"

OAJF 3239   :30
SEPTEMBER 15, 1982

1. (MUSIC UP)
(SFX: COOKING SOUNDS)

2. KID: What are you doing?

3. (SFX: COOKING SOUNDS CONTINUE) DAD: I'm making us French Toast.

4. KID: That's not...

5. ...how Mommy makes it.

6. DAD: Well, Mommy's not here.

7. (SFX: COOKING SOUNDS - PLOP)
(SFX: CHAIR PULL - CREAK)

8. (SFX: DOOR OPENS)

9. (INSIDE FREEZER VIEW)

10. (SFX: COOKING SOUNDS)

11. (SFX: TOASTER SOUNDS)

12. (SFX: COOKING SOUNDS)

13. KID: This is how Mommy makes it... DAD: (DOES DOUBLE TAKE)

14. ANNCR VO: For your toaster, or microwave. Aunt Jemima French Toast.

15. DAD: Just like mommy makes.

J. WALTER THOMPSON COMPANY

J. WALTER THOMPSON, 1979

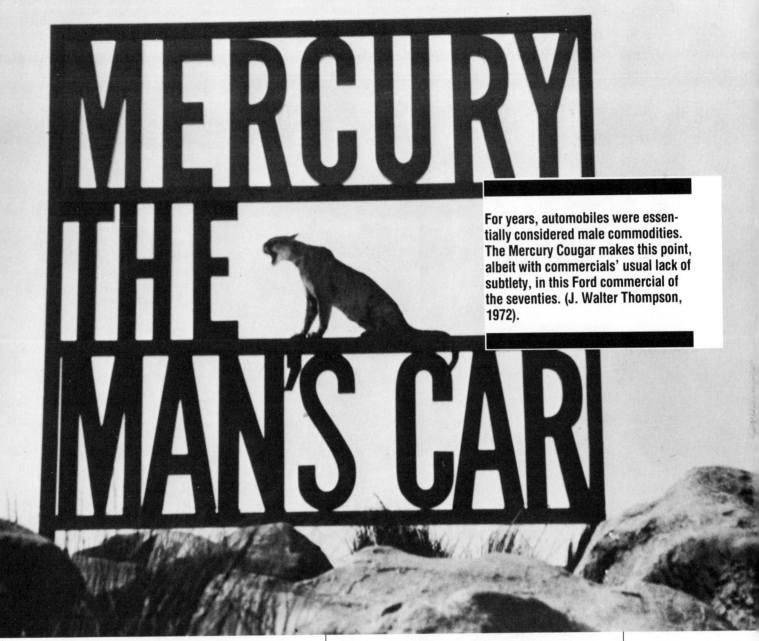

MERCURY THE MAN'S CAR

For years, automobiles were essentially considered male commodities. The Mercury Cougar makes this point, albeit with commercials' usual lack of subtlety, in this Ford commercial of the seventies. (J. Walter Thompson, 1972).

One well-executed commercial with this theme was a comedy for Aunt Jemima French Toast titled "Father and Son." The script, a creation of the J. Walter Thompson agency, features a harried young executive in tie and pinstriped vest who makes a mess of the kitchen as he struggles to cook breakfast for his son. Surveying the carnage of broken eggshells, the boy says doubtfully, "That's not the way Mommy makes it." The father replies ruefully, 'Well, Mommy's not here."

Viewers, having witnessed a similar scene in 1979, in the movie *Kramer vs. Kramer*, assumed the husband was upset because his wife had abandoned them. "This is a real-life situation done believably," says Elizabeth Harrington of Quaker Oats, which now owns the Aunt Jemima Company. "The wife is not supposed to be dead or divorced, she's just away." The woman has seen to her family's needs, though, by stocking the fridge with frozen French toast. The boy heats these up in the toaster while his father fumbles with the griddle. And then, like all precocious children in commercials, he presents the completed breakfast to his startled father.

A Kid Vid variation on the contemporary father and son relationship, produced by Malt-O-Meal cereal in 1982, employed a philosophy that has become a tradition in the films of Walt Disney. Children are shown to be invariably smarter than adults, and also more imagina-

malt-o-meal co.

1520 TCF TOWER • MINNEAPOLIS, MINNESOTA 55402 • PHONE 612/338-8551

Product: Malt-O-Meal Hot Wheat Cereal
Code No./Title: XMFC8202/"Funny Bear"
Date: August 1982   **Length:** 30 Second F/C

1. FATHER: Hey, what happened to your cereal?

2. SON: AH-H-H. . .A big bear took it.

3. FATHER: Oh. . .Lucky bear, cuz that was Malt-O-Meal. . .

4. smooth and creamy wheat;. . .

5. toasted malt; iron fortified;. . .

6. Good Stuff Maynard!

7. SON: Can I have some?

8. FATHER: Sure, but why don't you show me that bear first?

9. SON: Are you sure you want to see it?

10. FATHER: Umhum. SON: O.K.!

11. FUNNY BEAR: More Malt-O-Meal, please. FATHER: Maynard, close the door.

12. (Anncr VO): Malt-O-Meal Hot cereal, A nice part of a nutritious breakfast.

MARTIN-WILLIAMS, 1982

tive. Parents, while benign, are stuffy and un-enlightened. In the Malt-O-Meal ad, this theme was played out at the breakfast table. A father demands of his son, Maynard, "What happened to your cereal?" "A big bear took it," Maynard replies. When the father asks to see the bear before giving his son more cereal, the child opens the kitchen door, and, sure enough, a seven-foot grizzly is there, holding out an empty bowl in his paws, begging, "More Malt-O-Meal, please!" Doomed to his conventional world, and unable to accept the inexplicable, the father can only say, "Maynard, close the door."

THE REIGN OF THE GOOD OL' BOYS

The heartiest, happiest, and most self-satisfied men in commercials appear in beer ads. These are the men seen rafting down Coor's Colorado rapids, or hoisting their mugs in a Pittsburgh tavern, singing "From one beer lover to another, Strohs!"; the ones enjoying a Lowenbrau on a camping trip with the toast, "Here's to good friends!" The male equivalent of Clairol's declaration for women—"If I have but one life to live, let me live it as a blonde!"—is the Schlitz campaign of the early seventies: "You only go around once in this life, so you have to grab for all the gusto you can get."

But the best buddies, toughest good ol' boys, and most virile working men—all popular male images of the late seventies and early eighties—appeared in commercials for Miller Beer. Miller High Life was originally an elitist brew, "the Champagne of Bottled Beers," served only on special occasions. But when Philip Morris acquired the Miller Brewing Company of Milwaukee in 1970, it spent ten years broadening the beer's appeal, targeting its ads toward eighteen-to-thirty-four-year-old males, who are the nation's leading beer consumers. The initial campaign, "If You've Got the Time, We've Got the Beer," promoted Miller as a mellow reward at the end of the hard day's work, focusing on blue-collar workers. The rousing "Welcome to Miller Time" jingle ushered in the next series of commercials, which featured cowboys, longshoremen, cabdrivers, firemen, and other working men who

call it quits at sunset and invade their local taverns for their favorite brew. Beautifully photographed and exciting to watch, the Miller ads were later stylistically echoed in the campaigns of competitors, most successfully in Budweiser's popular "This Bud's for You" commercials.

Miller rose to an even more difficult challenge when it encouraged macho consumers to drink Miller Lite. A good-tasting, low-calorie beer did not exist before the seventies, and the very idea was ludicrous to most male beer drinkers. In a survey, one respondent claimed that ordering a light beer would be "like John Wayne swaggering into a bar and ordering a Pink Lady." But who would argue with football giants like Bubba Smith, Dick Butkus, and Ben Davidson?

Miller drummed in the message that Lite "tastes great" and was "less filling" by employing "America's best-known beer drinkers," like writer Mickey Spillane and coach John Madden. The thirty-five well-known sports figures used as spokesmen in the ads would split into rival camps: those who insisted that Miller Lite's chief attribute was its taste, and those who appreciated the beer as "less filling." Push invarialby led to shove, and then to mayhem, with comedian Rodney Dangerfield sweating it out in the middle. The only women to appear in these ads were portrayed as dizzy blondes whom Spillane brought along to pour his beer. The entire troupe of spokesmen assembled in "The Vote" to poll for the most popular spokesman, and again in 1982's "Alumni Bowling" and 1983's "Alumni Baseball" to settle their differences in slapstick "matches of the century." Each attempt at brotherhood led inexorably to pandemonium.

The jocks of the Miller Lite ads were tough guys with senses of humor, and good drinking buddies who often were intense rivals on and off camera. (The scene in which Yankee owner George Steinbrenner fires his manager, Billy Martin, for the umpteenth time, could hardly be called satire.) And they were a fair representation of how most men of the time would like to imagine themselves—palling around through life with strong arms, good laughs, and stalwart friends. The ideal world depicted in beer commercials shows the way to have a great time with none other than one's closest buddies.

HIGH LIFE BEER

"SEAPORT"

COMM'L NO.: MOML 3130

LENGTH: 30 SECONDS

Song: Welcome to Miller Time,

It's all yours,

and it's all mine.

Bring your thirsty self right here,

you've got . . . the time,

We've got the beer . . .

for what you have in mind,

Welcome to Miller Time . . .
Yours and Mine.

ANNCR: (VO) The *best* beer for the best time of the day.

ANNCR: (VO) Miller High Life!

AMERICA'S BEST KNOWN BEER DRINKERS TALK ABOUT **Lite** BEER...

COMM'L NO.: MOTK 0930

TITLE: "ALUMNI BOWLING"

JONES: Deacon's my name, and bowling's my game.

MADDEN: Gutter Ball! Gutter Ball!

BUTKUS: (VO) How you going to score that?
MARTIN: Come on, three strikes and you're out.

HEINSOHN: We just won another round of Lite Beer from Miller.

RED AUERBACH: Well, Lite sure tastes great!

CROWD: LESS FILLING!!! TASTES GREAT!!!

POWELL: Hold it! Hold, it, Jim.

You're going the wrong way. There it is down there.

MIZERAK: Eight ball in the pocket.

BUTKUS: Hey Bubba, this ball doesn't have any holes in it.

SMITH: Now it does.

MEREDITH: The score is all even.
NITSCHKE: Last frame. Who's up?

CARTER: Rodney...

CROWD: RODNEY???
BUTKUS: Got to be a mistake.

DANGERFIELD: Hey you kidding. It's a piece of cake.

DAVIDSON: All we need is one pin Rodney.

ANNCR: (VO) Lite Beer from Miller. Everything you always wanted in a beer. And less.

MADDEN: I didn't get my turn yet. I'm gonna break this tie.

Chapter Four

Sex in
Commercials

"Take
Take it

Television viewers pay attention to sexy ads. Sponsors heed this fundamental fact and produce sexy ads, while always denying that their commercials are salacious. Their messages are, according to advertisers, "stylish," "entertaining," and "provocative." Sponsors are sensitive to charges of selling with sex, since sex on network television

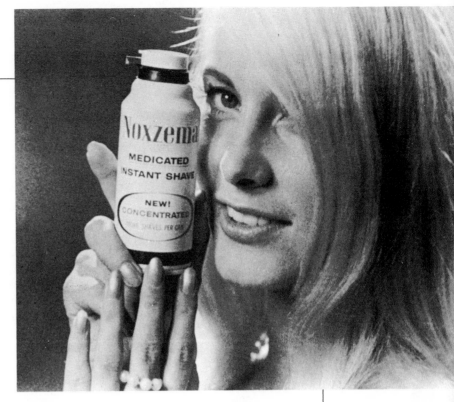

it off.
<u>all</u> off!"

continues to be the perennial red-herring issue. (The real crime is vapid programming.) Each network has its "standards and practices" department, which reviews sponsors' commercials and judges their acceptability. Networks prefer their in-house censors to the threat of external censorship, and though commercials today are more frank and

free than ever, the nervous networks are still inclined to bring down the curtain on advertisers that are too bold and bawdy.

The notion that European or Japanese television commercials are sexier than ours is another popular misconception. Taken en masse, foreign video ads are weak and diffuse when they are not browbeating the consumer with the hard-sell, which most do. To break through to inattentive viewers, overseas advertisers unschooled in the art of compacting humor and sentiment into thirty-second time slots sometimes resort to R-rated nudity. Such glimpses of skin, bright and salutory as they may seem to us, are more sophomoric than erotic. The Europeans do excel with suppleness and nuance of style that show up in the occasional glimmering moments in their commercials. English director Ridley Scott attempted to capture the mood of the better European ads in his sexually symbolic Chanel No. 5 commercials (discussed on page 99).

SIRENS OF THE EARLY YEARS

Sex in advertising dates back beyond the turn of the century. Attractive Gibson Girls were used in the 1900s to sell Coca-Cola. During the fifties, television advertisers were usually content to present a comely model as an attention-getting "stopper." Kissing, except in animated commercials, and references to sexual acts, were taboo. But occasionally, commercials with sexual themes were produced. These seem all the more remarkable today because they were anomalous, given the antiseptic nature of other contemporary commercials. One was aired in the mid-fifties by Snarol, the snail-killing insecticide. Titled "Garden," it showed two snails, a couple of lecherous thugs, moving in to molest a pair of female daisies. The pretty flowers huddle in each other's petals in fear. But out of some Snarol pellets scattered on the lawn arises a smoky siren. Wiggling an enticing finger, she coaxes the snails over to her. Lured by her "tantalizing aroma," they drool over the grass, only to be beaten to death with a mace by the curvaceous female phantom.

The first lady of TV commercial sex, Edie Adams, began her long reign in 1960. Before

A rare sado-erotic commercial from the early fifties was "Garden" for Snarol. (circa 1954)

"Hey, big spender, spend a little dime on me," sang seductive Edie Adams for Muriel Cigars. (Lennen & Newen, 1965)

Adams suggestively sang, "Hey, big spender, spend a little dime on me," her sponsor, Muriel Cigars, had fallen on hard times. Sales had drastically decreased. Muriel's first commercials of the fifties featured an animated cigar with Mae West's face and insinuating voice. Edie Adams was recruited to play essentially the same type of character in the flesh. Adams's first appearance for Muriel was on her husband's hit television program, *The Ernie Kovacs Show*. A rival cigar manufacturer, Dutch Masters, sponsored Kovacs's show, but needed to sell off some surplus commercial time. An account executive at the Dutch Masters ad agency phoned a friend at Muriel's agency and, as a joke, offered the commercial slots. Muriel called his bluff and bought into the program. Then, to heighten the irony, Kovacs's wife was hired as Muriel's singing and dancing spokeswoman.

Edie Adams's hip-grinding, sultry-voiced performances were goodnatured but provocative. She was seen singing the Muriel jingle in Broadway-style production numbers shot in a jazz nightclub, a Western rodeo, and other settings. Adams was the first of the great, attention-getting "stoppers," as sexy spokeswomen are known, and she helped Muriel's sales to regain lost ground.

In 1962, another siren wiggled out of a tube of Brylcreem in perhaps the most erotic commercial ever aired. In a misty, dreamlike setting, the mystery woman with her come-on smile and tight dress snuggled up to her victim. Saxophones wailed while she took off the man's glasses, unfastened his tie, ran her fingers through his hair, and planted a steamy kiss on his lips, the longest kiss ever to appear in a

MURIEL *Coronas*

The Noxzema Girl urged men to "take it off, take it *all* off!" (William Esty, 1966)

One of commercials' most startling and amusing images featured a svelte temptress wiggling out of a tube of Brylcreem. (Kenyon & Eckhardt, 1962)

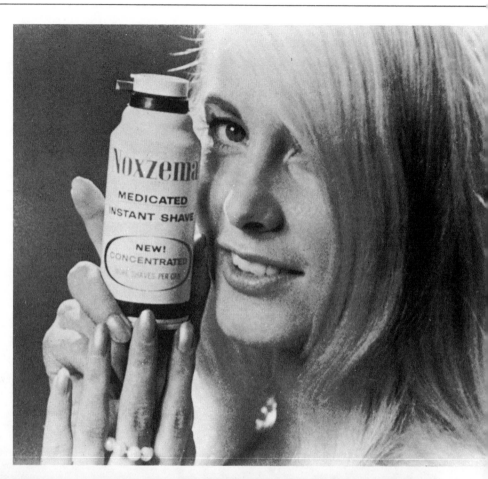

commercial. Smoke obscured the scene, and when it cleared, the temptress broke from the man's embrace long enough to challenge the camera in a husky whisper: "Brylcreem. Are you man enough to try it?"

SEXY PITCHWOMEN OF THE SIXTIES

A comely Swedish blonde came on the air in 1966 and purred, "Take it off. Take it *all* off!" Immediately after her command, a hot rendition of George Rose's pop hit, "The Stripper" played to accompany the teasing strokes of a razor against a man's chin. He shaved off the cream in neat, clean rows, "stripping" his face to the beat of the music. "The closer you shave," sang the blonde, "the more you need Noxzema." Having pouted and cooed through the ad, tossing suggestive glances at the camera, she concluded by caressing an aerosol can, and then the cheeks of the clean-shaven man.

The Swedish actress, Gunilla Knutson, was all of eighteen years old when she first seduced viewers in Noxzema's commercials. The William Esty advertising agency had been unable to find a woman with the proper cool yet steamy appeal. When Gunilla arrived one day to audition for a detergent commercial, the Noxzema account men immediately took to her. Her "Stripper" ads eventually numbered fifteen, with contemporary sports figures like Carl Yazstremski appearing in cameos to get "stripped" by Gunilla look-alikes. In one ad, an actress asked, "Ladies, want to see Joe Namath get *creamed?*" as she fondled the face of the New York Jets quarterback. Noxzema's business tripled. Knutson's come-ons prompted Rhode Island Senator John Pastore, chairman of the Senate Subcommittee on Communications, to urge TV's Code Review Board to prevent such "egregious sex" from ever going on the air. That the Noxzema Girl's ads were playful and tongue-in-cheek made the prospect of misguided censorship chilling.

While the Noxzema Girl was hot, some thought Joey Heatherton was hotter. She was sultry as she lay atop Serta mattresses in her gowns that resembled negligees, and caressed the springs to demonstrate their responsiveness (yes, they would rise right up beneath her touch). Serta's mattress would lift Heatherton like a magic carpet into the sky and spin her through a surreal dreamscape of whirling daisies and misty backdrops. It was these hallucinatory "trips" of the early seventies in which the kittenish Heatherton was most memorable. The former nightclub performer and perennial TV variety show gamine also appeared in Vegas-like production numbers for her sponsor. In a voice both husky and sweetly inviting, she sang, "Serta—the perfect sleeper."

The networks' standards and practices departments were concerned about what they considered Heatherton's "erotic dancing." They were also upset at the symbolism associated with the mattress, not to mention the amount of cleavage exposed. "But the real heat in those commercials came from Joey's performances," says Tom Prchal, then an account executive for Serta at the D'Arcy McManus & Masius agency, which created the ads. "Joey was a quiet and unassuming woman who would show up on the set in blue jeans and sweaters. But when the crew put on the playback music and the cameras began to roll, she really came alive! It's as if someone had given her a magic potion."

CHANGING EROTICISM FOR THE SEVENTIES

Heatherton sang and gyrated until the recession of the mid-seventies brought hard-sell commercials back into vogue. Serta then adopted a new strategy, promoting the value of its product as the "Sleep Machine," and Heatherton, not being an engineer, could hardly be expected to speak credibly about the mechanics of a mattress. By 1979, however, the time was right for another sexy spokeswoman, and Tom Prchal, now president of the Don Tennant Company, Serta's new agency, brought in actress Susan Anton. "Physical fitness chic" was sweeping the country, and Anton appeared in a jogging suit in her commercials to proclaim, "The Serta Perfect Sleeper—it's a healthy investment in yourself." The mattress was now part of a regimen for good health that consisted of exercise, proper nutrition, and rest. Anton's advice was sensible, but a lot less fun than the sexy movements of Heatherton.

SERTA PERFECT SLEEPER-1972
TELEVISION SPOTS
"JOEY HEATHERTON - WATERFALL"

(MUSIC UP & UNDER) JOEY SINGS: Be a perfect sleeper. Buy a Perfect Sleeper.

Perfect Sleeper by Serta.

The mattress made like no other in the world.

Perfect Sleeper by Serta.

Now instead of counting sheep you can count on a good night's sleep.

JOEY: (LIP SYNCH) Hi, I'm Joey Heatherton. And you can be a perfect sleeper too.

On that wonderful Perfect Sleeper Mattress by Serta.

It's made like no other mattress in the world.

You'll love it . . .

Serta Perfect Sleeper.

Something great to sleep on. JOEY SINGS: Be a perfect sleeper. Buy a Perfect Sleeper. Perfect Sleeper by Serta.

Available in:
60 Seconds (PS-TV-91)
30 Seconds (PS-TV-92)
20 Seconds (PS-TV-93)

D'ARCY-MACMANUS & MASIUS, 1969

"What you're looking for in a 'stopper' is a hot property. Connie Stevens was a hot property. Suzanne Somers was a hot property," says Ed Cummings, director of advertising for Ace Hardware. He goes on to explain how the two sex symbols of the seventies were chosen to represent, of all things, a chain of hardware stores: "It's the oldest trick. The first thing you have to do is get the viewer's attention."

Connie Stevens, a star of Las Vegas and several television variety shows, spun around in a sequined gown in her commercials and sang, "Ace is the place with the Helpful Hardware Man," beginning in 1974. She was replaced in 1978 by Suzanne Somers. After singing the Ace jingle, both women deferred to the Helpful Hardware Man, an actor named Lou Fant. Stevens and Somers would also have fun teasing the shy Hardware Man, caressing his cheek and cooing in his ear. Before Stevens went on the air, only one out of four consumers had ever heard of the sponsor's hardware chain. Three out of four were "Ace aware" by the end of Somers's reign in 1982.

When Edie Adams completed her long-running stint as spokeswoman for Muriel Ci-

Sexy Santa Suzanne Somers replaced Connie Stevens to become Ace Hardware's next "stopper." Although the sponsor was rattled when *Playboy* magazine printed some R-rated photos of Somers—sexy spokeswomen cannot be *too* sexy—the brouhaha passed and the actress continued to sing, "Ace is the place with the Helpful Hardware Man" until 1982. (D'Arcy McManus & Masius, 1978)

Susan Anton is in dreamland atop a Serta. (Don Tennant Company, 1979)

Serta
Perfect Sleeper
"It's a healthy investment in yourself!"

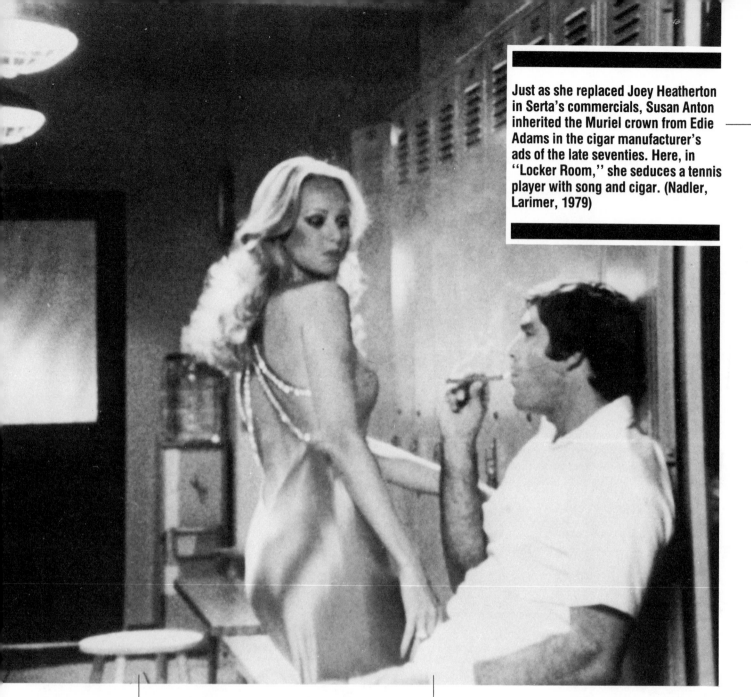

gars, three actresses—Jan Daley, Margaret Davis, and Susan Anton—competed to be the new Muriel Girl. The public cast its ballots as part of a promotional sweepstakes and Susan Anton was chosen. Anton's most provocative Muriel commercial, in 1976, had her appear in a men's locker room. Wearing a strapless silk dress and glistening diamonds, she seduced a spellbound tennis player with a song and a cigar.

The viewers of NBC's *Today* and *Tonight* shows were exposed in 1974 to what at first glance appeared to be a typical glamour commercial for a woman's product. As the camera lovingly passed across a pair of shapely legs, a female announcer intoned: "The following com- mercial will prove to the women of America that Beautymist Panty Hose can make any legs look like a million dollars." Discriminating viewers noticed a hefty bulk to the model's clean-shaven legs, while others grew curious when the camera panned up past a pair of green silk shorts and a New York Jets football jersey bearing the number 12. At last the dim- pled face of quarterback Joe Namath came into view. With a twinkle in his eye, Namath said, "Now, I don't wear pantyhose. But if Beauty- mist can make *my* legs look good, think what they can do for yours."

"Was that *really* Joe Namath wearing panty hose?" asked Johnny Carson when the ad was first aired on his program. Indeed it was. This

Beautymist makes any legs
look like a million dollars.
Even Joe Willy's.

ANNCR: The following commercial will prove to the women of America

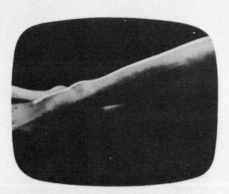

ANNCR: That Beautymist Panty Hose can make any legs

ANNCR: look like a million dollars.

JOE: Now I don't wear Panty Hose. But if Beautymist can make my legs look good, think what they'll do for yours.

ANNCR: Somehow everything looks better through Beautymist.

ANNCR: Especially your legs.

beautymist

"The Wella Girl," Farrah Fawcett-Majors, poses with a bottle of her sponsor's product. (Creamer Advertising, 1974)

off-the-wall advertising idea resulted from the meticulous strategy of Hanes Hosiery and its agency, Long, Haymes & Carr of Winston-Salem, North Carolina. They wanted to position mid-priced Beautymist against popular economy brands and high-priced rivals. When the commercial aired, Beautymist's name recognition among consumers soared 100 percent. Joe Namath's lucrative career as a TV pitchman also took off. Norelco paid him $10,000 in 1969 to shave off his Fu Manchu mustache with the company's cordless electric razor. The quarterback's agent was soon entertaining an assortment of six-figure offers to have his client endorse products. Namath, the top male sex symbol at the time, was seen in ads for Hamilton Beach, Fabergé, Arrow Shirts, and his own line of men's clothing. He earned more in ads than he ever did playing football. But the Hanes Beautymist commercial was his only memorable effort. Hanes benefited from a deluge of free publicity, and the commercial became a staple in every comedian's repertoire.

There was a time in the mid-seventies when no college man's dorm room would be complete without a poster of Farrah Fawcett-Majors wearing a clinging red swimsuit. Five million posters were sold, a record that went

unchallenged until it was surpassed by E.T. in 1982. Fawcett's trademark on the poster and in her hit television series, *Charlie's Angels*, was her prodigious blond hair, for the actress had been known for years as "The Wella Girl."

The Wella Corporation of Englewood, New Jersey, was looking for a single spokeswoman back in 1974 to do ads for its diversified beauty products and "give them continuity," according to Thomas Chilakas, the company's advertising director. "We interviewed fifteen women, gave them scripts, and put them in front of the camera with a bottle of Wella Balsam Conditioner. The most outstanding was this beautiful blonde with stunning hair, a wonderful smile, and a twinkle in her eye. Everyone wanted to know who she was." Wella invested huge sums of advertising funds promoting their spokeswoman, and the company was paid back handsomely when her poster and TV show solidified Farrah Fawcett-Major's sex-symbol image. Never taking herself too seriously in her commercials, she would smile broadly, speak softly, and shake her massive hairdo. Even after Fabergé hired her in the late seventies and brought out a line of Farrah Fawcett beauty products, she was still entrenched in the minds of consumers as "The Wella Girl."

Man by Jōvan Woman by Jōvan
"One Man and One Woman."
30 Second-Color

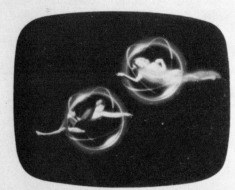
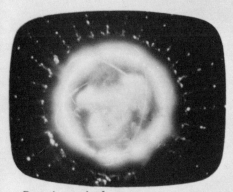
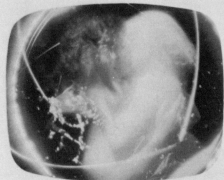
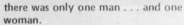

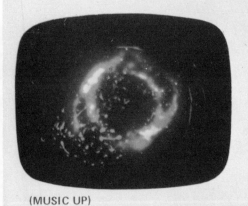

(MUSIC UP)

ANNCR: (VO) In the beginning,

there was only one man . . . and one woman.

Now there still is.

MAN by Jovan - - the most masculine aftershave/cologne ever.

WOMAN by Jovan - - the concentrated essence of total femininity.

Experience the fragrances.

Then experience the timeless feeling that there is

but one man - - and one woman - - in all the world.

SYMBOLISM AND FANTASY FOR THE EIGHTIES

After the sexually combative seventies, a more sanguine sensibility in male–female relations came about in the early eighties. The sexes needed each other now. Jovan's 1981 ad, "One Man and One Woman," introduced the unisex fragrance Man and Woman. A toga-clad couple float through space, at one point duplicating Michaelangelo's Sistine Chapel fresco in which God reaches out to Adam, while the announcer intones: "In the beginning there was only one man and one woman. Today there still is."

One of television's sexiest half-minutes: the Paco Rabanne "Man in Bed." (Ogilvy & Mather, 1981)

The ad was created as a counterpoint to the independent Charlie, who needed no one else in her life, and the values that were beginning to reassert themselves following the "sex wars" of the sixties and seventies.

Paco Rabanne cologne's "Man in Bed" commercial was one of television's sexiest half-minutes. On the screen, a sultry, French-accented man stirs himself awake as the telephone rings. Spotting a note pinned to the pillow next to him, he reads it, smiling, while crossing his bedroom/artist's studio. Paintings and discreet camera angles disguise his nudity.

"Hello?" he yawns into the phone.

"You snore," an affectionate woman's voice informs him.

"And you steal the covers," he responds jokingly. His naked torso seen only from the waist up, the man whispers to his lover that he'll miss her while she's away in San Francisco.

The ad agency Ogilvy & Mather cast French actor François Marie Bernard in the title role of this unconventional commercial. A two-page print ad showing Bernard in bed, with the commercial's sexy dialogue expanded and printed alongside, appeared in *Vogue, Esquire,* and other publications just prior to the

CHANEL N°5
"SHARE THE FANTASY" - REV.

Director: RIDLEY SCOTT
Music: VANGELIS

(MUSIC THROUGHOUT)

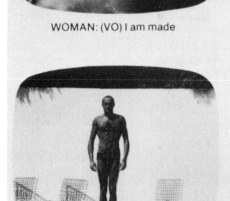
WOMAN: (VO) I am made

...of blue sky

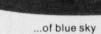
...and golden light

...and I will feel this way

...forever.

MALE: (VO) Share the Fantasy.

CHANEL N° 5

With their emphasis on the slim and youthful, diet soft drink ads are some of the most scintillating currently on the air. Diet Pepsi offers us a peek into a sorority room. Downstairs, the boys stand agape. A pretty girl winks in the last scene: ''Sip into something irresistible.'' (BBD&O, 1983)

air date of the television commercial. The ad contributed to the sensation that occurred once the commercial was finally seen. The Paco Rabanne man became the fantasy figure of the year, although he appeared only during the principal cologne-selling seasons of Father's Day and Christmas. As a promotional stunt, department stores around the country hired actors to lie in beds placed in store windows, with extension phones placed on the sidewalk so passersby could call. ("Are you wearing anything under those sheets?" "Is that accent for real?" "What are you doing tonight?") Ogilvy & Mather was swamped with requests from women's groups for copies of a commercial that, to them, represented advertising's new portrayal of the sexes: It is the woman now who rises at dawn to go on a business trip, leaving the hunk to languish in bed. Like all "sexy" commercials, "Man in Bed" made its point with style and humorous tone that kept the censors at bay and viewers eager for more.

Another fragrance, Chanel No. 5, employed surreal imagery to create its visually exciting, sexually charged "Share the Fantasy" commercials. At $120 an ounce, Chanel was not offering the fantasy to just anybody, and this upscale appeal was emphasized in the elegant commercials crafted by the Doyle Dane Bernbach agency. English director Ridley Scott used the same studied, impeccable composition and atmosphere that made his feature films *Alien* and *Blade Runner* visual feasts.

"Share the Fantasy" begins with a shot of a chateau in the South of France. Cool, synthesized music is heard, performed by Vangelis, the composer who was later responsible for the

Academy Award-winning music for *Chariots of Fire*. An airplane silently glides over the chateau's roof. Beside a blue swimming pool, a woman drops her robe and sits, exposing her naked, tapered back to our view. Her eyes close and her lips part as she reclines. The plane's shadow passes lengthwise over the pool and directly over the reclining woman. A man appears at the opposite end of the pool, materializing out of thin air. Silently he dives into the water and swims toward her beneath its surface. He is the airplane incarnate, with his arms outstretched—a mythical figure, perhaps nothing more than the woman's daydream. Her voice is heard: "I am made of blue sky and golden light, and I will feel this way forever." The man emerges from the pool. The woman sits up and spreads her legs to greet him. He disappears. The woman lies down again, resigned. Shadows pass over the pool.

The sequel to the 1980 commercial was also directed by Scott. But 1982's "Gardens" is a confused homage to artists as diverse as René Magritte, Salvador Dali, and Andy Warhol. The sequel fails to spark the magic of the original, a milestone in erotic commercials.

Advertisers will continue their forays into sexual adventurism in commercials to enhance the allure of their products. The current flesh peddlers of note are the diet soft drink ads, which seek to capitalize on the continuing national craze for "physical fitness," an ideal that seems to be at odds with soft drinks of any caloric content. Whether shot on the beach or in the bed, we can be certain that commercials will always rely on "the oldest trick" as the proven lure.

Chapter Five

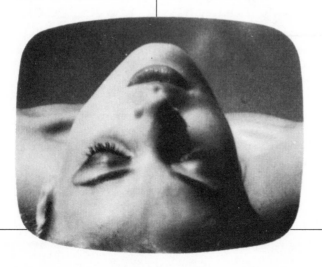

Kid Vid
Commercials

"Oot-fray,

Some of television's most ingenious commercials are seen by only a minority of viewers, those preadolescents who tune in to Saturday morning's children's TV programming, known as "Kid Vid." The average child watched six hours of television a day in 1982. That adds up to forty thousand hours of television by the time the child is eighteen. The same child would have spent only eleven thousand hours in the classroom. So, while children enjoy their Kid Vid fantasies, parents, educators, and sociologists are concerned about TV's influence on the lives of young Americans. They are also concerned and critical about

Oops-lay!"

kiddie commercials as well. "As a psychological matter," says Peggy Charren, founder of the private consumer group Action for Children's Television, "children are cognitively incapable of understanding all television commercials directed toward them."

During television's early "anything goes" years of the fifties, sponsors routinely showed children acquiring superhuman strength by eating breakfast cereals, or leaving their friends choking in a cloud of dust kicked up by the sponsor's sneakers. Special film effects were used to make a toy seem larger, faster, and more "lifelike." It was not until

1977 that the Council of Better Business Bureaus formed the Children's Advertising Review Unit. The board's report, "Children's Advertising Guidelines," set down a list of thirty "Can't Do's," including a caution to sponsors against using special effects to enhance a toy's appearance and operation. Kid Vid advertisers were also told not to foster certain ideas in impressionable minds, such as the suggestion that a child will gain prestige or a special skill by owning a product, or the implication that a parent is a good parent if he or she purchases the product.

BARBIE AND THE CENSORS

The evolution of television advertising for children can be traced in commercials for Barbie, the svelte fashion doll introduced in 1957. Barbie is the best-selling children's toy of all time and is made by the Mattel Company of Hawthorn, California. Barbie was originally portrayed in the Mattel ads as less a doll than a glamorous female ideal surrounded by soft music, breathless announcers, and sets that gave no indication how small she really was. For an immobile mannequin, this little gal really got around. Barbie was shown in a nightclub, where she was a "singer," in a hospital as a nurse, in a church as a bride, and in the nation's capital, where she resembled Jackie Kennedy. Often, several Barbies would gather to

model outfits together. Young girls yearned for Barbie the way they saw her on TV. They were disappointed when they could neither obtain all of Barbie's clothing and accessories, nor duplicate her commercials' theatrical effects at home.

Barbie's commercials have changed significantly since her early days. Mattel is one company that takes its social responsibilities seriously (it was the first toy company to stop manufacturing toy guns), and it responded to the consumer complaints. Barbie is now seen exclusively in the hands of little girls, usually in "natural" settings like a girl's bedroom or playroom. And the doll is truthfully shown to be as large as she actually is—which, as any little girl, past or present, knows, is precisely eleven and three-quarters inches tall.

HEROES AS HUCKSTERS

Over the years, the tremendous affection children have for their Kid Vid heroes has been compromised when the stars of children's programs have doubled as pitchmen, pitch-animals, and even pitch-aliens for products. Children implicitly trust the characters on TV. They watch attentively as current characters like Fred Flintstone shout, "Yabba-dabba-do!" for Cocoa Pebbles cereal or when Spider-Man swings from a web to demonstrate the potency of his vitamins. But in the nonregulated fifties,

Barbie is outfitted by her Mattel fashion designer. The most popular doll in the world introduced little girls to sophistication and fashion in toys when she made her first appearance in 1957. Barbie's initial commercials reflected that ''adult'' appeal. (Ogilvy & Mather, 1957)

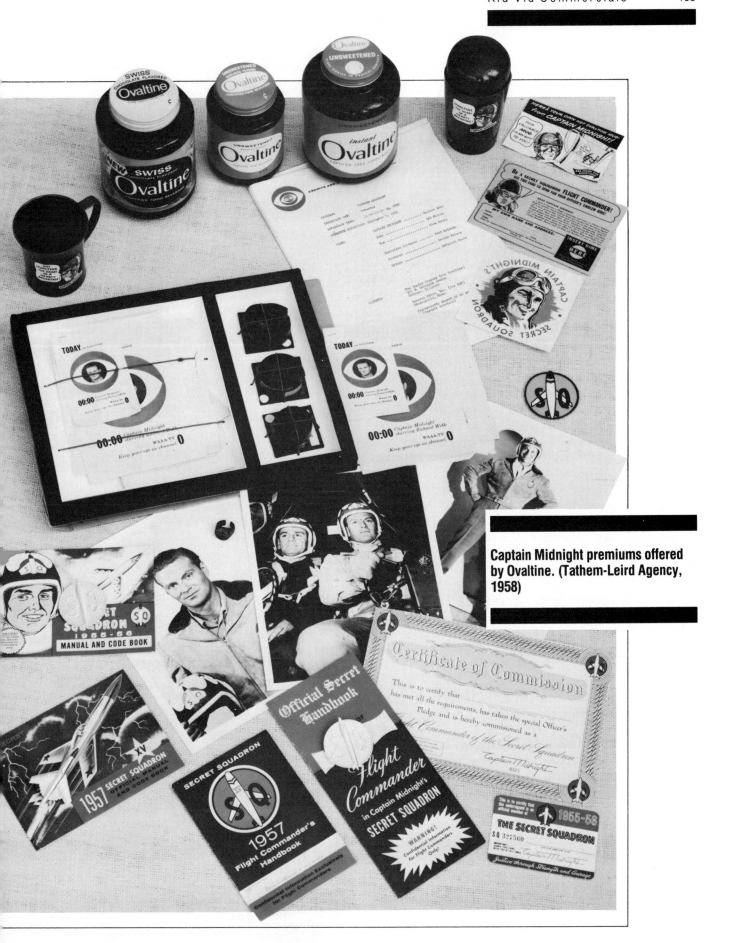

Captain Midnight premiums offered by Ovaltine. (Tathem-Leird Agency, 1958)

Kid Vid stars would interrupt their programs to endorse toys, cereals, and candies as a matter of course. Captain Midnight, Howdy Doody, and even everyone's favorite pedagogue, Miss Frances of *Ding Dong School*, all sold Ovaltine.

The fifties were the golden age of premiums and no one offered more than Captain Midnight. As portrayed by firm-jawed Richard Webb, Captain Midnight originated on the radio in 1940, then appeared from 1952 through 1959 on CBS television. The character had received his name when, as Captain Albright, he returned from a secret wartime flying mission at the stroke of midnight, which "saved the Allied cause." With the return of an ever-tenuous peacetime, Captain Midnight was designated SS-1, leader of the Secret Squadron, which "assisted federal authorities in fighting injustice throughout the world," especially against archvillain Ivar Shark. Ovaltine, the show's sponsor, found that premiums that allowed children to participate actively in the show were the best way to build up viewer loyalty. Kids received Secret Squadron badges and code rings by sending in jar labels, a clever way to sell Ovaltine, and a gimmick that the sponsor had originated in the thirties on the *Little Orphan Annie* radio show. Captain Midnight would flash a series of numbers in the middle of a day's adventure. These could only be deciphered by using a premium ring. A typical Secret Squadron message of the day: "3-7-17-5-22/11-20-5-25-9-17-5-10." Translation: "D-R-I-N-K O-V-A-L-T-I-N-E."

THE CARTOON ID CHARACTERS OF KID VID

Fresh-Up Freddie, Seven-Up's identifiable Kid Vid character of the fifties, was Walt Disney's first venture into television commercials. Disney had become a producer of children's programming in 1955 with *The Mickey Mouse Club*. For *Zorro*, Disney's other popular show of the time, the studio was commissioned to create the commercials for the sponsor—Seven-Up.

An anthropomorphic rooster, cocky and bright, Fresh-Up Freddie gave lessons on how

Fresh-Up Freddie assures Kid Vid viewers, ''Nothing does it like Seven-Up!'' (Leo Burnett, 1959)

to throw a successful party or stage a "bang-up" picnic. His commercials were classic Disney, beautifully animated and full of gags. When Freddie wanted to add "plenty of laughs" to a party, he grabbed a jar of "Canned Laughter" off a shelf containing "Chuckles," "Giggles," and hysterical "Ha-Ha's." He would fill the room with so many balloons, the house would break away from its foundation and float into the sky, its escaping balloons, silhouetted against the moon, resembling the bubbles of the carbonated soft drink. Freddie personified Seven-Up's happy slogan: "You Like It/It Likes You!"

Along with Tony the Tiger and Snap! Crackle! and Pop!, Sugar Pops Pete was one of the earliest animated ID characters to promote a cereal for the Kellogg Company of Battle Creek, Michigan. A prominent advertiser in children's television, Kellogg has long enjoyed the ability of its agency, the Leo Burnett Company, to concoct popular identifiable characters. Burnett promoted Cocoa Krispies cereal during the fifties with Coco, a talking cartoon monkey who declared: "It tastes like a chocolate milkshake, only crunchy!" Coco was followed by Tusk! Tusk! the Elephant, then the venerable trio, Snap! Crackle! and Pop!. Froot Loops® debuted early in the sixties with Toucan Sam®, a colorful spokesbird that sounded like Ronald Colman. He made popular the pig-latin jingle, "Oot-fray, Oops-lay!" Also during the sixties, Yogi Bear, Huckleberry Hound, Snagglepuss Tiger, and other animated stars from the Hanna-Barbera Studio appeared together in commercials for Kellogg's Corn Flakes®. This was after Kellogg's rooster, Cornelius, had crowed his last sales pitch.

Kellogg's Kid Vid gang lines up for a 1958 family portrait: Tony the Tiger (Frosted Flakes), Coco (Cocoa Krispies), Snap! Crackle! and Pop! (Rice Krispies), Sugar Pops Pete (Sugar Corn Pops), Smaxie (Sugar Smacks), and Cornelius (Kellogg's Corn Flakes). (Leo Burnett, 1958)

Reunited twenty-five years later, the new Kellogg's family includes Toucan Sam (Froot Loops), Snap! and Crackle! (Rice Krispies, Cocoa Krispies, Frosted Krispies, Strawberry Krispies), Poppy (Corn Pops), Tony the Tiger (Frosted Flakes), Dig 'Em (Honey Smacks), Tony Jr. (unemployed, formerly Frosted Rice), and Pop! (Leo Burnett, 1983)

Rejoicing over his breakfast cereal, a boy sings what was perhaps the most famous Kid Vid jingle: ''Sugar Pops are Tops!'' (Leo Burnett, circa 1953)

Sugar Pops Pete sweetens a box of his cereal with his candy-striped ''Pop Gun.'' Pete was the first of a long line of Kellogg's ID characters created expressly for Kid Vid. Their images would then adorn the product boxes. In his commercials, Sugar Pops Pete would go up against, and in the end ''sweeten,'' opponents like Billy the Kidder and the malicious newspaper editor Bad News Daily. (Leo Burnett, circa 1958)

But it was the long-running "Sugar Pops Are Tops!" jingle that had children sitting up and singing along. Sugar Pops Pete was a stylized ground squirrel with an enormous ten-gallon hat and a Western twang. In his ads, the Wild West was fraught with villains and varmints like the evil newspaper editor, Bad News Daily, and the outlaw, Billy the Kidder, who, according to the narrator, was "so bad he wouldn't even help his mother with the dishes!" "Can't, Ma!" Billy would holler as he left the house. "Gotta go rob a bank!" Instead, Billy ran into Sugar Pops Pete and got himself shot with sparkling sugar dust from Pete's candy-cane-striped "pop gun," making him as sweet as the cereal.

"We never condescended to kids," says Rudi Perz, who wrote many of the Kellogg's ads at Burnett. "In fact, because we had to sell the stories to the client, they were written to make *adults* laugh." The contemporary Kellogg's commercials still make us laugh because of the richness of their visual puns and imaginative scripts.

Another Western character, Marky Maypo, began his Kid Vid adventures in 1958. The popular little cartoon boy who fancied himself a rough-and-ready cowboy refused at first to eat the sponsor's product. "Cowboys don't eat cereal," he announced, crossing his arms and curling his lips into a pout. Trying to convince his nephew, Uncle Ralphie would swallow a spoonful. His eyes would light up and he would begin gobbling up the stuff until a

Robbed of his cowboy hat and his favorite cereal by his Uncle Ralphie, Marky Maypo wails, "I want my Maypo!" His cry was repeated by Kid Vid fans at breakfast tables all over the country. John Hubley animated this classic. (Brian & Houston, 1958)

jealous and frustrated little Marky would shout out Kid Vid's most famous line: "I want my Maypo!"

Good and Plenty's Choo-Choo Charlie, the Casey Jones of Kid Vid, at the throttle. The "Choo-Choo Charlie" jingle was another standard from the hit parade of children's video ads. Charlie showed his viewers how to rattle the box of licorice candy to imitate a train engine's "chugging" sound, and how to blow through the empty box to make it whistle. These effects were usually duplicated by his fans in darkened movie theaters, typically during love scenes. (Bauer & Tripp, 1960)

Marky's first commercial in 1959 ran for years, until the Standard Milling Company of Kansas City produced a sequel. In "Marky's Horse," Uncle Ralphie snores on the sofa, oblivious to his nephew's pleas that he wants his Maypo. Finally the little cowboy jumps on his uncle's pot belly and rides it like a bronco. Marky's cousin appeared in a new commercial in 1962. She was an emaciated beatnik who slinked around on limbs of rubber. Marky stared at her as if she had just dropped in from another planet. This oddball household, a Kid Vid fixture through the mid-sixties, managed to hold itself together by a shared passion for the maple-flavored cereal.

Choo-Choo Charlie was the Casey Jones of Kid Vid. Sitting alone in a chair, the freckled animated boy with the enormous engineer's hat announced, "All aboard!" and began to simulate the sound of a chugging engine by rattling his box of Good and Plenty. His passengers were his dog and a little girl dressed in her mother's floppy hat, dress, and high heels. Whenever she'd steal one of the pink and white Good and Plenty candies from Charlie's box, he complained, "Aww, you're eating my engine!"

The former president of Philadelphia's Quaker City Chocolate and Confectionery Company, Lester Roscum, recalls that in 1959, "I wanted to create a character who was totally believable and had all the characteristics of a

real kid. He had to be an interesting little boy, with a huge imagination."

The UPA Studio animated the first Choo-Choo Charlie commercial and created its sequel, which shows the intrepid engineer in the cab of an actual, albeit cartoon, locomotive. His theme song is sung by a chorus of male balladeers: "Choo-Choo Charlie was an engineer/ Choo-Choo Charlie had a train we hear/He had an engine and he sure had fun/He used Good and Plenty candy to make his train run!" Then Charlie's girl friend picks up the refrain.

Choo-Choo Charlie disappeared in the mid-sixties. But the Switzer Candy Company of St. Louis, which acquired Good and Plenty in 1982, plans to bring him back to entertain a new generation in the near future.

Sibling rivalry was never better portrayed than in the "Winners Warm Up with Malt-O-Meal" ads of the early sixties, featuring Little Freddie and his nameless Older Brother. Three of commercials' top animators, Ray Patin, who directed, and his protégés Gus Jeckle and Jim Murakami, created the commercial at Playhouse Pictures in Hollywood. Based on the Campbell-Mithun agency's script by Don Grawert, the first of the Malt-O-meal series began in May 1960. Freddie humiliated his boastful older brother with the strength and speed he acquired through eating Malt-O-Meal—"like spinach powers Popeye," according to the memo that outlined the ad agency's original

Freddie and his older brother warm up with Malt-O-Meal. (Campbell-Mithun, 1960)

strategy. While Older Brother made bumbling attempts to demonstrate how to swing a baseball bat, shoot an arrow, or lift a barbell, Freddie gobbled down his Malt-O-Meal, then proceeded to shoot the bow like an expert marksman, twirl the barbell like a baton, and swat the baseball bat so hard it splintered. When Older Brother played make-believe astronaut, imagining a flight to the moon, Freddie spun his cap and actually flew into the stratosphere, though his brother complained, "Freddie, you aren't even supposed to cross the street!"

"We couldn't show that today," says Leo Pontius, vice-president of marketing and advertising for the Minneapolis-based Malt-O-Meal

Punchie winds up, preparing to give Oaf a "nice Hawaiian Punch." This was the longest-running gag in all of television. (Atherton-Privett, 1960)

Company, "because they show a kid obtaining superhuman strength. All Malt-O-Meal is, is a hot cereal of one hundred calories." Here, perhaps, Kid Vid regulators go too far. Those who remember Freddie's commercials from their childhood never took them literally, any more than they took Popeye literally. To kids they were funny!

The most devious question heard in the schoolyard playgrounds of the sixties and seventies was the one that a cartoon character named Punchie posed to an ever-gullible Oaf: "Hey! How about a nice Hawaiian Punch!" Woe to the child who innocently answered, "Sure!" as Oaf always did. Punchie would wind up and deck the doltish Oaf, who resembled a stereo-

typical tourist, with one roundhouse blow. Kids found this slapstick gag irresistible; it was repeated thousands of times over two decades.

The original "Punchie and Oaf" ad was created in 1960 by Alfred Atherton, president of the Atherton-Privett agency. (He advised his producers to eat crackers to avoid ulcers, the common advertising profession malady.) John Urie, who had invented the Western Airlines bird and would later direct ads for Goodyear, Levi's, and Vicks cough syrup, took Atherton's concept and came up with the Punchie and

Oaf characters. The famous twenty-second cartoon was made, but Hawaiian Punch had no money to buy television time. Urie recalls, *The Tonight Show*, with Jack Paar, was then the cheapest time you could buy. It was a late-night, sophisticated show and absolutely the wrong place to advertise a household product bought by mothers for kids. But when it aired, Paar took a look at it and said, 'Let's run that again!' And they ran it again, free. Three days after the commercial was shown, you couldn't buy a can of Hawaiian Punch in New York. Then Atherton decided to buy a whole minute on *The Tonight Show*, but we only had this one twenty-second commercial. He asked me, 'What'll we do?' I said, 'Show it once in the beginning, show a picture of the can for twenty seconds, then show it again.' We did, and it was sensational!"

Punchie and Oaf eventually left the late-night sophisticates and became two of the most familiar residents of children's television.

The longest-running gag in children's television continues to be the Trix Rabbit's devious attempts to taste Trix cereal. In his black-and-white debut in the fifties, he introduced himself: "I'm a rabbit, and rabbits are supposed to like carrots. But I hate carrots. I like Trix!" Thus began his efforts, now going on for thirty years, to trick children into giving him a taste. "Silly rabbit, Trix are for kids," he is constantly reminded by the children he attempts, without success, to dupe.

When the Rabbit disguised himself as a coal miner or a cowboy and managed to obtain

The sheepish Trix Rabbit looks as if he has just been caught stealing Trix cereal. Like Kellogg, General Mills designs popular ID characters to advertise its cereals and to appear on its product boxes. The Trix Rabbit, after conniving for years, was finally given a bowl of "raspberry red, lemon yellow, and orange orange" when kids voted in his favor in a 1976 election. (Dancer, Fitzgerald & Sample, 1976)

Bill Tollis, an art director at the Dancer, Fitzgerald & Sample agency, which helped develop the Trix Rabbit, participated in a creative meeting in the early sixties where an identifiable character for a new cereal, Cocoa Puffs, was born. While Tollis sketched, writer Gene Cleaves said, "We have this bird. A cuckoo bird." Cleaves elaborated, "And he says, 'I'm cuckoo...I'm cuckoo for Cocoa Puffs!'" Another writer, Jack Keil, broke into a maniacal dance, flailing his arms and shouting at the top of his voice: "I'M CUCKOO FOR COCOA PUFFS! I'M CUCKOO FOR COCOA PUFFS!" Keil was so enthused that he demonstrated the character, screaming and kicking, atop the boardroom table at General Mills, suitably impressing the startled client. In the Cocoa Puffs commercials, the loony Cuckoo Bird, named Sonny, went crazy whenever his foil, a bearded bird named Gramps, tormented him with the sight of his favorite cereal. Network programmers of children's television shows considered the Gramps character "too mean," and he was dropped. Today, Sonny interacts with live children, but he still explodes with Jack Keil's original enthusiasm over a bowlful of Cocoa Puffs.

In 1963, the S.S. *Guppy* sailed into Kid Vid, beginning a series of adventures of Cap'n Crunch cereal that continue to this day. In his first appearance, the *Guppy*'s skipper, with his white walrus mustache and blue Napoleonic hat, assured his viewers that the Quaker cereal "has to be good because they named it after me!" The *Guppy* sailed with a crew of four children—pony-tailed Brunnhilde, bespectacled Alfie, gap-toothed Dave, and little Carlyle, who never spoke—plus a canine first mate named Seadog. The ship went from the deserts of Mesa Land, where the spotted Crunchberry

a bowlful of cereal, he would invariably be exposed when, in his excitement, his headgear flew off and his large ears popped out. As tenacious as Charlie the Tuna, he would be back to try again in the next commercial. Kid Vid viewers grew to share the Rabbit's frustration; the four-foot-tall Trix Rabbit, not an adult but a likable "big kid," was too nice to be continuously foiled. Perhaps realizing that his parable might teach a damaging lesson—try as you may, you will never achieve your goal—General Mills found a way out of the situation. During the 1976 presidential elections, a campaign was held in the Trix commercials. Mailing in box-top ballots, young viewers decided either "yes," the Rabbit will get his Trix, or "no," Trix is still exclusively for kids. Over 99 percent of the ballots were pro. As balloons fell and a brass band played, the Rabbit finally tasted his Holy Grail, and went berserk with ecstasy. Then, like Oliver Twist, he held out his empty bowl and asked for more, only to be told to wait until the next election.

Cap'n Crunch, the skipper of the S.S. *Guppy.* (Ad Com, circa 1970)

Jay Ward's original sketch of the "first" Quake, horsing around here with his rival, Quisp. Quake, the superhero, and Quisp, the alien, each had his own cereal to plug, and their competition became so intense that Kid Vid viewers expressed fears that Quake would catch the propeller-topped mite and "stomp" him. (Ad Com, 1965)

Quake, revised and less intimidating. (Ad Com, 1969)

Beast raised his strawberry-flavored crunchberries to the African forests, where a friendly elephant, Smedley, sporting a Cap'n Crunch hat and a peanut-colored hide, sought out the cereal's peanut-butter-flavored variety. In these commercials, everyone is crazy for the cereal, and in the best-executed episode, "Breakfast Aboard the *Guppy,*" the ship is invaded by everyone from cross-country bicyclists to Martians, all eager to try Cap'n Crunch cereal. But no one was as voracious as a pirate named La-Foote, who conspired throughout the series to steal the *Guppy*'s precious cereal cargo.

The Cap'n Crunch cartoons were long on visual humor. "Children are primarily visual until they are nine or ten," explains Elizabeth Harrington of the Quaker Oats Company. "They experience the world through pictures before they can read. And they really don't become comfortable with advertising or capable or receiving messages until they are eight or nine." For these reasons, Jay Ward Productions was commissioned to create the series. Ward's animated programs for children, including the immortal *Rocky and Bullwinkle,* with its "Fractured Fairy Tales" cartoons, and *George of the Jungle* contained sophisticated messages and mature satire that was appreciated by kids and adults alike. Some of the most attractive animation to emerge from the Ward studio in Hollywood has been the Cap'n Crunch commer-

cials, and some of filmdom's finest voice-over talents, all old Jay Ward alumni, played the roles. Daws Butler, the voice of Huckleberry Hound and Yogi Bear, does the Cap'n, and June Foray, heard as Rocky the Flying Squirrel and Mrs. Smurf, does Brunnhilde. William Conrad narrated the early episodes.

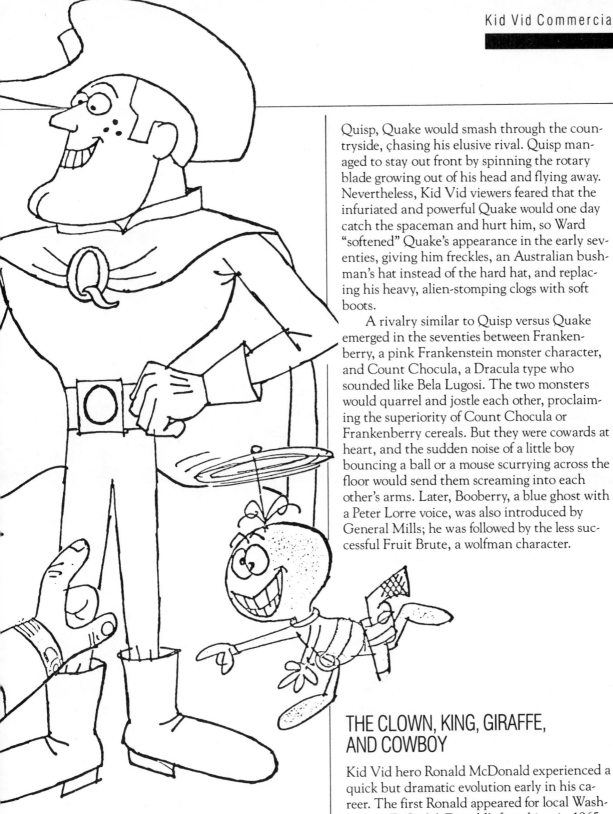

Quisp, Quake would smash through the countryside, chasing his elusive rival. Quisp managed to stay out front by spinning the rotary blade growing out of his head and flying away. Nevertheless, Kid Vid viewers feared that the infuriated and powerful Quake would one day catch the spaceman and hurt him, so Ward "softened" Quake's appearance in the early seventies, giving him freckles, an Australian bushman's hat instead of the hard hat, and replacing his heavy, alien-stomping clogs with soft boots.

A rivalry similar to Quisp versus Quake emerged in the seventies between Frankenberry, a pink Frankenstein monster character, and Count Chocula, a Dracula type who sounded like Bela Lugosi. The two monsters would quarrel and jostle each other, proclaiming the superiority of Count Chocula or Frankenberry cereals. But they were cowards at heart, and the sudden noise of a little boy bouncing a ball or a mouse scurrying across the floor would send them screaming into each other's arms. Later, Booberry, a blue ghost with a Peter Lorre voice, was also introduced by General Mills; he was followed by the less successful Fruit Brute, a wolfman character.

THE CLOWN, KING, GIRAFFE, AND COWBOY

Kid Vid hero Ronald McDonald experienced a quick but dramatic evolution early in his career. The first Ronald appeared for local Washington, D.C., McDonald's franchises in 1965. Attired in a shapeless costume, with french fries bulging from his pockets and his hat serving as a rack to hold soft drinks, Ronald would not speak because the clown who played him had a thick Russian accent. The second Ronald was played by another clown, Washington weatherman Willard Scott, who later became

Conrad also created the voice for the character Quake, another Jay Ward creation from the mid-sixties who pitched his namesake Quake cereal. Quake found his attempts to sell his cereal mocked and interrupted by a little green alien named Quisp, who was out to advertise his own brand, Quisp cereal. Teased by

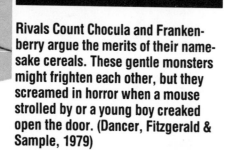

**Rivals Count Chocula and Franken-
berry argue the merits of their namesake cereals. These gentle monsters
might frighten each other, but they
screamed in horror when a mouse
strolled by or a young boy creaked
open the door. (Dancer, Fitzgerald &
Sample, 1979)**

The Today Show's meteorologist. And the
Ronald for Kid Vid viewers in Chicago was Ray
Raynor, star of several Windy City children's
programs. But it was not until the Needham,
Harper & Steers agency hired actor King
Moody in 1970 that the definitive, national
Ronald came into being.

Ronald and his friends cavorted in Mc-
Donaldland, an Oz-like fantasy forest where
bushes grow burgers, and brooks flow with
soda pop. The fiendish Hamburglar plotted his
mischief in this colorful land—actually a film
set in Los Angeles the size of a football field,
where dozens of Ronald's ads were shot each

year—but he was always foiled in the end.
Ronald and the gang concluded their commercials by dining on the patio of a make-believe
McDonald's. For kids, it was indeed "your kind
of place." Adults would rarely see the Mc-
Donaldland commercials, which were shown
on prime time only during the *Peanuts* specials
and other family specials. As a result, adults
had little concept of Ronald's immense popularity among children. Screaming throngs greeted
him at franchise openings, and even the shyest
child opened up when the clown made one of
his regular hospital visits. (The Ronald Mc-
Donald Houses, built next to hospitals to ac-

commodate the families of young patients who have to endure extended convalescences, represent one of the most acclaimed community-service programs ever initiated by a corporation.) Children regularly write to Ronald with their problems. Some personal letters dealing with family tragedies and the traumas of growing up are so delicate that special care is taken by the McDonald's Corporation of Oak Brook, Illinois, to see that each is promptly answered by specially trained counselors. Such is the faith that kids place in their video friends, particularly the affable adult clown with the fire-engine-red hair who is associated with what is probably America's most popular food.

Ronald McDonald greets his Kid Vid fans. As played by King Moody, the ubiquitous clown ruled over the colorful fantasy world of "McDonaldland," as well as appearing at franchise openings from coast to coast, where parents were astonished by his popularity among children. (Needham, Harper & Steers, 1970)

Another popular Kid Vid character who is almost wholly unknown to adult viewers is the Burger King King. The King began his reign for the "Home of the Whopper" in the late seventies in an attempt to counter Ronald Mc-Donald. The King is a magical monarch, and from his first appearance in 1976 he has performed tricks like levitating onion rings and making himself disappear into the air of a Burger King restaurant. The "magic" theme, perceived by creative strategists as having a universal appeal for all ages, lends the ads a unity not always found in those of the King's rival, Ronald. These commercials, by the J. Walter Thompson agency, managed to double Burger King's recognition factor among children within the King's first six months on the air, and today they have brought it to parity with mighty McDonald's.

Burger King's magic King casts a spell. Created as a rival for Ronald McDonald, the King had a distinctly nonderivative personality. (J. Walter Thompson, 1976)

During the last three months of every year since the early seventies, Geoffrey, the seven-foot-tall Toys 'Я' Us giraffe, his wife Gigi, daugher Baby Gee, and, since 1980, son Junior, have emerged from the print advertising they appear in throughout the year as cartoons and are seen as real-life identifiable characters on children's television. In "Roller Disco," Geoffrey and his family skate about a strobe-lit dance floor with other long-necked patrons. "Hoedown" features the giraffes square-dancing in a country barn. They are seen riding bicycles, playing tennis, and involving themselves in other "real-life situations," according to a company spokesman. "Kids think of the giraffes as real people. They love running up to Geoffrey when he's making an appearance at a hospital or a store opening and giving him a hug."

What the giraffes will not do is actually sell products. Whenever they enter a Toys 'Я' Us store in a commercial, they are shown as regu-

lar shoppers, customers like any human. This has put them in the good graces of parents and Kid Vid critics, who are pleased that the popular giraffes are corporate representatives and do not abuse their influence by making sales pitches for toys and games. Children recognize the difference, as well. Says a Toys 'Я' Us spokesman: "When they write to Geoffrey, it's not as if they're writing to Santa, asking for things. They want to know how Baby Gee and Junior are, and what it's like living in a lighthouse."

Soft bubble gum was introduced in the sev-

enties by Beechnut/Life Saver's Bubble Yum, followed in 1977 by Warner-Lambert's Bubblicious with its transcendental claim, "It's the Ultimate Bubble with the Ultimate Flavor," a claim that might have been considered too grandiose by even the most uncritical child viewer. But Wrigley's late entry, Hubba Bubba (a delightful nonsense name originating in the forties zoot-suiter's expression, "Hubba-hubba!"), took on the market with its popular commercials and unique product claim: When the Hubba Bubba bubble breaks, the residue won't stick to the blower's face. This technolog-

ical breakthrough was first touted in "The Gum Fighter." The 1979 commercial was the first of a series of Western spoofs starring Don Collier, whom trivia experts recognized as Clint Eastwood's trail boss on *Rawhide*. Production values—the authentic sets, costumed extras, period locomotives, etc.—were some of the highest for any Kid Vid commercial, though costs were held down by filming in Old Tucson, a collection of permanent Western movie sets in the Arizona desert.

The Gum Fighter was consistently challenged in his commercials to *High Noon*-style shootouts with many villains chewing other brands of gum. Facing each other, the Gum Fighter and the bad guys would blow larger and larger bubbles until these exploded, to the gasps of onlookers. The challengers were so disfigured by the sticky goo of their lesser gums that they hid their faces from the camera, while the Gum Fighter neatly peeled his off and blew on the wad as if it were a smoking Colt pistol. Then he would speak his only line: "Big bubbles. No troubles!"

The Gum Fighter made Hubba Bubba so popular that Wrigley's could not manufacture enough, and stores in whole regions of the country ran out of stock. In 1980, special commercials were produced for these areas. In one, the Gum Fighter rides into town and, by advising patience, holds off an angry mob besieging the general store, telling them, "It'll be a long time" before they see their Hubba Bubba again. These ads kept demand high for a product that could not even be purchased by children—a unique strategy that inculcated many young viewers to the market realities of supply and demand.

THE REAGAN IDEAL: A NONREGULATED INDUSTRY

In March 1982, a federal court judge ruled that the National Association of Broadcasters' Television Code, which, among other caveats, prohibited sponsors from advertising more than one product per one-minute commercial, was an illegal restraint of trade. Like the Council of Better Business Bureaus' Children's Advertising Guidelines, which are directed toward ad-

"Big bubbles. No troubles," promised Hubba Bubba's Gum Fighter. In his elaborately produced Western spoofs, the Gum Fighter would be challenged to *High Noon*-style shootouts with ever-expanding bubbles of gum as weapons instead of six-shooters. (BBD&O, 1979)

vertisers, the NAB's Television Code, intended for broadcasters, was voluntary, but was respected by TV stations throughout the United States. Rather than change the offending element of its code, the NAB dropped its entire list of guidelines, thus creating a vacuum that will permit broadcasters to run more commercials during Kid Vid programs, as well as to broadcast ads for hard liquor, which is now being done in some states—and, conceivably, commercials for firearms.

Also in 1982, after twelve years of contemplating the Kid Vid scene, a special task force of the Federal Communications Commission was disbanded without having made any recommendations about children's advertising on television. As a result, a private consumer group, Action for Children's Television, has become the sole video watchdog against what it finds to be deceptive and, in the case of unhealthful foods and unsafe toys, dangerous Kid Vid commercials. Fortunately, the ACT, whose diverse support organizations include the National PTA, the NAACP, and the UAW, is vigilant, responsive, and dedicated to the welfare of over forty million current Kid Vid viewers. Nor are all advertisers villains, either. Such companies as Mattel Toys and Malt-O-Meal have shown responsibility as they adapt their commercials to changing sensibilities.

With luck, all Kid Vid sponsors will live up to their responsibilities, or possibly face censorship if they do not. As endearing as the jingles, jokes, and identifiable characters of child-oriented ads have proved to be among young viewers, they represent the most powerful, and now unbridled, sales tools on television, and are ripe for misuse. In the absence of federal or industry regulations for Kid Vid ads, American parents have little choice but to put their faith in the integrity of the sponsors and the common-sense wariness of their video-addicted children.

Chapter Six

Humor and Innovation

"Try it, You

THE HUMORISTS

Most television commercials are collaborative efforts among the creative staffs of advertising agencies. An idea will often originate with the sponsor. A film production company is then given a script and storyboard, which is the scene-by-scene comic-strip "blueprint" of the completed commercial, and is instructed to "shoot the board." In theatrical filmmaking, the director is often a czar. In commercials, the director is usually an accomplice.

Then there is Stan Freberg. Since the mid-fifties, companies eager to enhance their advertising with the "Freberg touch" have given the satirist a free hand to do essen-

'll like it!"

tially whatever he wants, which often turns out to be spoofs of other advertising. Freberg accepts TV commercial jobs when he is not producing records or films. He writes, directs, edits, and produces all his own ads, the only man in commercials to wear all four hats.

Freberg's specialty is giving a boost to unknown firms by using imaginative and often bizarre ads and promotional stunts. "All the little underdog companies came to me for recognition. They were invisible. I made them visible. My philosophy is that most advertising is audiovisual wallpaper. It's there but you don't really see it.

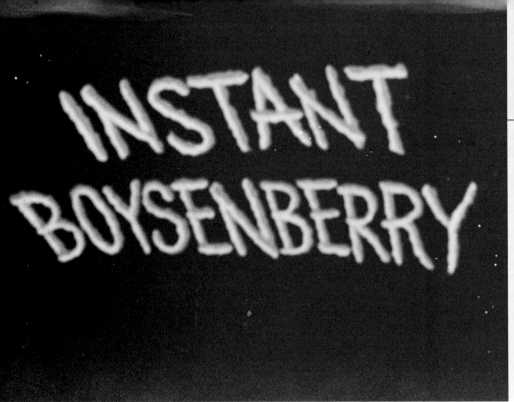

"When I start writing, I begin with the assumption that people are already leaving the room. You have to do something interesting, fast." In Freberg's very first commercial campaign, in 1956, for Contadina tomato paste, he established himself as an iconoclast with a jingle that broke all the rules—it never once mentioned the sponsor's name. "Who put eight great tomatoes in that itty-bitty can?/You know who, you know who, you know who!" And after a slight pause, Freberg's voice intoned, "In case you don't, its Contadina Tomato Paste."

Butternut Coffee was sold primarily in the Los Angeles area, though not much was sold. In 1958, Freberg was hired to give Butternut a higher profile. He hit upon the idea of running a series of commercials Monday through Friday at the same time and over four L.A. television stations simultaneously. Viewers who flipped their dials in any direction would tune into Stan Chambers, a familiar newscaster from KTLA, a local television station. "I wanted people to ask, 'What terrible national disaster is happening?'" recalls Freberg, who had also placed newspaper ads the day before that announced: "Tomorrow night, 10:30 P.M. Aviation's Outstanding Moment of the Decade!" Radio ads also trumpeted the event, though the sponsor's name, Butternut Coffee, was not yet mentioned. "I wanted to wake up the city of Los Angeles like an ammonia towel slap across the face."

On Monday night, viewers were told, "For the first time! Skywriting on television!" Newscaster Chambers stood on an airport tarmac with an actor playing "Mr. Butternut," along with Butternut's family, and watched skywriter "Ace Jenkins" attempt to paint the night sky with the message "INSTANT BUTTERNUT COFFEE." Unfortunately, Jenkins, who was a cropduster of boysenberry fields, flies too low and suffocates the group with smoke. Coughing, Mr. Butternut says they'll try it again the next night.

"To give you an idea what a fiendishly clever thing this was," says Freberg, "we bought time on the radio the next day." Listeners heard the following exchange:

ACE JENKINS: But I'm a cropduster!

BUTTERNUT: Yes, but you flew too low. Tonight try it at thirty thousand feet.

ACE JENKINS: Thirty thousand feet! You can't spray boysenberries at that height and be effective!

Jenkins had his crop on his mind, evidently, because when viewers tuned in at 10:30 P.M. on Tuesday night, they watched, along with the Butternut family, as Ace wrote "INSTANT BOYSENBERRY."

"That's Butternut, not boysenberry!" Ace was scolded by his boss on the radio the next day. Mr. Butternut's pep talk continued, "We'll try it again tonight. Now go up there and write something your mother would be proud of!" So, on Wednesday night, Los Angeles viewers

The Lone Ranger confronts his nemesis, a representative from Lark cigarettes. Clayton Moore, as the Lone Ranger, emerged from retirement for this bizarre ad, as did Jay Silverheels, as Tonto. (Freberg, Ltd., 1968)

watched Ace inscribe the word "MOTHER" over the clouds. Thursday night was worse. The flustered Jenkins wrote, "INSTANT (I FORGET!)."

By Friday night, Mr. Butternut's family had abandoned him to go to a movie. Alone with the announcer, he nervously faced the sky. Ace managed to write the message, but reversed the "R" in Butternut. "Who cares!" shouted the jubilant sponsor. As a result of this unique series, Butternut's share of the Los Angeles coffee market soared fourfold.

"Honesty is my secret weapon—honesty almost to the point of embarrassment to the cli-

ent," says Freberg. For instance, the cornerstone of Freberg's classic Chun King campaign of the early sixties was the news that "ninety-five percent of the American people haven't bought our chow mein." (Not for long. Sales shot up to 50 percent after the ads ran, supporting Freberg's contention that "anyone can make funny commercials. The artistry, as far as I'm concerned, is to do funny commercials that *sell* products.")

The Chun King ads began the profitable patron-artist relationship between the company's tempestuous president, Jeno Paulucci, and Freberg. In 1968, Paulucci's product, Jeno's Pizza Rolls, gave Freberg an opportunity to vent some anger against an annoying commercial then on the air. "When I was a kid, I spent most of my waking moments listening to the radio. The Lone Ranger was a hero to me. He and Rossini were the only ones permitted to use the William Tell Overture, as far as I was concerned. Then along came Lark cigarettes and ripped off the music." The 1967 Lark ad that raised Freberg's ire demanded "Show Us Your Lark Packs." At a formal party in Manhattan,

Ann Miller sings and dances for Great American Soups in "The Big Production." A homage to Busby Berkeley's movie musical extravaganzas of the thirties, the ad featured commercials' largest set, a streamlined moderne marvel with four thousand leaping water jets. The set also had a twelve-foot soup can that rose from the floor as a dance platform for Miller; the ad was choreographed by Hermes Pan. (Freberg, Ltd., 1970)

elegantly attired aristocrats gamely held up their cigarettes like models on a billboard. In his "revenge" commercial, Freberg asks a similarly dressed group of Beautiful People to "Show Us Your Pizza Rolls," using the same music. Men and women reach into their tuxedo jackets and jeweled purses and pull out packages of frozen hors d'oeuvres. A man smoking Lark cigarettes challenges the host, "I'd like to talk to you people about that music you're using." Suddenly, a gloved hand slams down on his shoulder. Behind him stands Clayton Moore as the Lone Ranger, with Jay Silverheels as his sidekick, Tonto. "That's funny," the Lone Ranger says dryly, "I've been wanting to speak to *you* people about the same thing." Tonto inquires, "Have a Pizza Roll, *Kemo Sabe?*" and then stuffs his own pockets with the snacks. "Who was that masked man?" asks a *grande dame.* "I don't know," the host inevitably re-

plies. "But I wanted to thank him." The Lone Ranger rides away, shouting, "Hi-Yo Pizza Roll!" and leaves his "calling card," a silver bullet, gleaming next to a box of the sponsor's product.

"The Big Production," Freberg's musical-comedy epic of 1970 for Heinz's Great American Soups was, just as its title promised, a rousing homage to Busby Berkeley's choreography. In fact, nothing like it had been seen since the thirties. Freberg hired Fred Koenecamp, the Oscar-winning cinematographer of *Patton,* and brought in Hermes Pan, Fred Astaire's co-choreographer, to supervise the dance number. One of the largest sets ever constructed for a commercial was outfitted with four thousand fountain jets that would shoot colored water into the air on cue. To star in "The Big Production," Freberg hired Ann Miller because "she was the only star from that era, the thirties, who hadn't changed. She still looked fantastic!"

The commercial begins with a shopworn situation ripe for parody. A husband returns from the office and greets his wife, who is puttering around the kitchen. "Hi, honey, I'm home. What's for dinner?" "Great American Soups," his wife says offhandedly. Dubious, the husband asks, "Would you mind giving me that again?"

On that cue, Miller throws off her housedress and reveals a red-sequined outfit beneath. The walls fly away to expose a red, white, and blue Art Deco stage set, and Miller breaks into song: "Hey, mister, have you heard the news, from Broadway to the Loop/It's the Great American Soup..." Twenty-one chorus girls join her, the fountains gush, and Miller finds herself tapdancing with top hat and cane atop a twelve-foot-high soup can that rises out of the floor. Then, as the walls of her humble kitchen come back together, she twirls back into the arms of her husband. "Emily," he says dryly, "why do you have to make such a big production out of everything?"

Beginning in 1969, the "Neighbors" series for Gillette's Right Guard deodorant became a three-year comic soap opera that kept viewers eager for each new installment. Gillette's Agency was BBD&O. The setup was simple: A wimpy man named Sidney, played by Bill Fiore, moves into a new apartment and discovers he must share his bathroom medicine cabinet with a jolly, nameless neighbor, played by character actor Chuck McCann. McCann greets the surprised Sidney with a garrulous "Hi, guy!" and then snatches away Sidney's Right Guard. "One shot and I'm good for the whole day!" he shouts as he breaks into a flamenco step. The long-suffering Sidney turns from his eccentric neighbor at the end of each commercial and whines, "Mona!"

In the ad's first sequel, Sidney's wife, Mona, enters the bathroom, refusing to believe they share a cabinet with the couple in 2D. But when she opens the door, she is greeted by the neighbor's wife, Janet, who burbles, "Gee, you have beautiful towels." The two women begin to argue over the ownership of the Right Guard can on their shared shelves, and the fight is not resolved until a policeman arrives to restore peace during the third episode.

In the fourth commercial, Sidney's son Howard opens the cabinet door and finds his neighbor's pretty daughter, Valerie. Love blooms with all the alacrity necessary in a thirty-second TV commercial. But as their fathers keep pushing past them to grab the Right Guard, Valerie laments, "We've got to stop meeting like this." However, in commercial number five, they are still seeing each other, if only in the bathroom. An argument ensues over whose father is to blame for interrupting their cabinet rendezvous. Howard is called away by Sidney. When he returns, he impulsively reaches through the cabinet and pinches not Valerie's cheek but her father's. He gets pinched right back by the affable neighbor. "Ha! Ha!" You're Mona's kid, aren't you? Is your dad in?"

Finally, one morning, the fat neighbor opens the cabinet door with his "Hi, guy!" greeting and finds himself face to face with a comely blonde, whom he assumes is Sidney's secret mistress. "Well, hello!" he says, taking her hands and covering them with kisses. "Does Mona know about you?" "Oh, they moved," the woman says cheerfully. "We're your new neighbors." Then she calls out, "Bruno!" A hulking giant lumbers into view to shock the contrite McCann character, who quickly releases the blonde's hand, no doubt wishing that old Sidney, who was so much fun, was back.

Viewers felt the same way. BBD&O retired the "Neighbors" commercials in 1972, only to revive them six years later. Once again, Sidney opens his cabinet to be tormented by an old face who is once more his new neighbor. This time McCann has a pudgy son who also swipes the Right Guard, perhaps a hereditary gesture. But one thing had not changed; Sidney still ended each ad with the plaintive cry, "Mona!"

A different approach was taken by General Telephone, the company its customers in West Los Angeles and the suburban San Fernando Valley loved to hate. Using its service was similar to telephoning in an underdeveloped country, with phones ringing by themselves, static blasting over the lines, and conversations whimsically disconnected. All told, the utility offered the Doyle Dane Bernbach agency its first opportunity to test, in TV commercials, a cinematic figure that had recently come into vogue: the antihero.

THE GILLETTE COMPANY
TOILETRIES DIVISION

LENGTH: 30 SECONDS

RIGHT GUARD

"ONE SHOT"

BBDO

COMM'L. NO.: GSGA 8073

McCANN: One shot and I'm good for the whole day.

FIORE: Oh . . . .

McCANN: Oh, Hi Guy . . . just tried your New Environmental Right Guard.

FIORE: My Right Guard?

McCANN: Heard this formula helps keep you dry and odor-free all day.

FIORE: So ?

McCANN: So, one shot and I'm good for the whole day.

FIORE: Again?

McCANN: Again?

McCANN: One shot and I'm good for the whole day.
FIORE: Mona . . .

Don't get dressed without it.

ANNCR: (VO) New Environmental Right Guard. Don't get dressed without it.

BBD&O, 1978

A "mea culpa" campaign was launched, in which the phone company admitted its ineptitude but pledged better service. In its commercials, all the pent-up frustrations felt by its customers were wonderfully vented. In one ad a wife urged her husband at a party: "Go on, Harry, say something funny." Harry's straight-faced reply: "General Telephone!" The partygoers burst out laughing, while a voice-over announcer added defensively: "We know some people think our service is laughable, but we're spending $200 million in California this year to improve it. What's so funny about that?"

than adequate service." A ripe tomato soars into the picture and clips the spokesman's chin. "But we're spending $200 million in California this year on improving our service." Unimpressed, someone pummels him with an egg. "Cables, switches, personnel, everything." The pièce de résistance, a cream pie, smacks him squarely in the face, leaving the man to sputter through the dripping custard, "Thank you for your patience."

The commercials dissipated some customer hostility, enjoyed some attention in the press, and even permitted the company to live on

Corporate angst in "Pass It On." Federal Express created a name for itself with humorous, sometimes off-the-wall commercials. In "Pass It On," the sponsor saved a corporation's employee from imminent unemployment. (Ally & Gargano, 1977)

But the most gratifying commercial featured a close-up of a conservatively dressed, middle-aged company spokesman. He self-consciously introduces himself, "Hello, I'm from General Telephone." The remark is met by offscreen hoots and catcalls. "Now, I'm aware that General Telephone provides less

borrowed time generated by public sympathy. That sympathy was short-lived, however, when it was discovered that $60 million of the promised $200 million in improvements was to come from a 40-percent rate increase. As a result, the "funny" General Telephone commercials became, in the end, instructive texts for public

guerilla action. Reports around Los Angeles in 1970 cited instances of people throwing vegetables at the company's service trucks.

Some of the oddest-looking people to appear in TV commercials have deadpanned their way through Joe Sedelmaier's hilarious Federal Express ads of the past ten years. Working out of his Chicago studio, Joe ("You have to entertain before you can sell,") Sedelmaier shuns slapstick in the commercials he directs in favor of the character-oriented comedy of Buster Keaton, who was an early influence. In his first national commercial, "Pass It On," the Federal Express classic from 1977, Sedelmaier spoofed the corporate chain of command. The ad follows the progress of an important package as it descends from the chairman of the board down to the mail boy. Each underling who receives the package is threatened by his superior, "If this package doesn't arrive in Peoria by tomorrow, it'll be *your* job!" Tension mounts. It appears the entire corporation will be fired if delivery is not made the next day. Happily, the easygoing shipping boy has the answer. He picks up the phone and casually sings, "Hello, Federal!"

"Pass It On" was written by Patrick Kelly and Michael Tesch of the Ally & Gargano agency, which had wanted to use Sedelmaier for Federal Express ever since the agency ac-

quired its client in 1974. But first, Federal Express, the overnight air-delivery service established in 1972 and considered by *Fortune* to be one of the top ten business successes of the seventies, ran two hard-sell campaigns to introduce its service and to lure some business away from Emery Air Freight, the industry leader of the time. Once these goals were met, Federal Express's marketing director, Vince Fagan, agreed to a new humorous approach in his advertising. One hit comedy followed another, enthralling viewers and winning every advertising award.

Probably the most memorable ad was "Fast-Paced World," a sixty-second commercial, a rare length in 1981, that featured an executive speed-talking his way through the day. At lunch, hiring an employee, conducting a board meeting, consummating a business deal on the phone, the executive speaks at a dizzying machine-gun tempo, representing, in an announcer's words, "this hectic, get-it-done-yesterday" business world. Only Federal Express, apparently, can keep up with him. The ad was designed for the unique talents of fast-talking actor John Moschita, whom the ad agency discovered on the *That's Incredible* TV show, where he demonstrated his skills. Sedelmaier peopled the ad with his usual supporting cast of oddballs, whom he discovers in the tav-

Ally & Gargano, Inc.
437 MADISON AVENUE, NEW YORK, N.Y. 10022
MURRAY HILL 8-5300

Client: FEDERAL EXPRESS CORP.
Product: AIR FREIGHT
Title: "FAST PACED WORLD"
Commercial No.: QFAS 1643 (:60)
Date Approved: 1/4/83

1. MR. SPLEEN: (OC)Okay Eunice,travelplans.Ineedtobein NewYorkonWednesday,LAon Thursday,NewYorkonFriday. Gotit?EUNICE:(VO)Gotit.

2. MR.SPLEEN: (OC)Soyouwant toworkhere,wellwhatmakesyou thinkyoudeserveajobhere?

3. GUY: Wellsir,Ithinkonmyfeet, I'mgoodwithfiguresandIhavea sharpmind.

4. SPLEEN: Excellent.Canyou startMonday? GUY: Yessir. Absolutelywithoutthesitation.

5. SPLEEN: Congratulation, welcomeaboard.

6. (SFX) (OC): Wonderful, wonderful,wonderful.Andin conclusionJim,Bill,Bob,Paul, Don,Frank,andTed,

7. businessisbusinessandasweall know,inordertogetsomething doneyou'vegottodosomething.In ordertodosomethingyou'vegot togettoworksolet'sallgettowork.

8. Thankyouforattendingthis meeting. (SFX)

9. (OC): Peteryoudidabang-up jobI'mputtingyouinchargeof Pittsburgh.PETER: (OC) Pittsburgh,perfect.

10. SPLEEN:Iknowit'sperfect Peterthat'swhyIpickedPitts- burgh.Pittsburgh'sperfectPeter. MayIcallyouPete?

11. PETER: Call me Pete.
SPLEEN: Pete.

12. SECRETARY: (OC) There'sa Mr.Snitlerheretoseeyou.

13. SPLEEN: Tellhimtowait 15seconds.

14. SECRETARY: Canyouwait 15seconds.MAN:(OC)I'llwait 15seconds.

15. SPLEEN: (OC) Congratulation sonyourdealinDenverDavid.I'm puttingyoudowntodealinDallas. Donisitadeal?Dowehaveadeal?It's adeal.Ihaveacallcomingin...

16. ANNCR: (VO) In this fast moving high pressure, get-it- done yesterday world.

17. (VO): Aren't you glad there's one company that can keep up with it all?

18. SPLEEN: (OC) Dickwhat'sthe dealwiththedeal.Arewedealing? We'redealing. Daveit'sadealwithDon, DorkandDick. Dorkit'sadealwith Don,DaveandDick.

19. Dickit'saDorkwithDonDealand Dave.Dave,gottago,disconnecting. Dorkgottago,disconnecting.Don gottago,disconnecting.Dickgotta go,disconnecting...

20. ANNCR: (VO) Federal Express. (SFX) When it absolutely, positively has to be there overnight.

When it absolutely, positively has to be there overnight.

erns and subway stations of Chicago.

Viewers used to seeing glamorous actors and models in commercials take notice when Sedelmaier's offbeat comedies come on the tube. In his Mr. Coffee ad, disgusted coffee drinkers toss their pots out their apartment windows to rain down by the dozen on a mailman who is protected from the metallic deluge only by an umbrella. A regional commercial for Southern Airlines follows a passenger from the spirited orgy in a rival air carrier's first-class section and back into second class, where he is greeted by peasants in babushkas and threadbare coats, who eat gruel and moan a lot. Despite the director's quasi-existential advertising philosophy—"advertising can't pretend to be anything but what it is"—Sedelmaier's work bears the signature of the most original comic commercial maker since Stan Freberg.

THE INNOVATORS

The paradox of television advertising is that even though it is a conservative business—production costs and air time are too expensive to take risks—the irreducible fact that television is an entertainment medium to which viewers turn to escape their quotidian boredom compels sponsors to seek out new ways to attract attention. As a result, television commercials have always been a source of filmic innovation. The computer-generated graphics of the TV ads of the seventies and eighties have been adapted to the other contemporary media, a "look" that is the signature of our time. The short scenes and rapid editing of the commercials of the sixties revolutionized the movies of that decade, which copied their techniques.

During the fifties, which was TV commercials' first decade, the exciting experimental work was being done in animation. Studios like Storyboard, Shamus Culhane, Playhouse Pictures, and Ray Patin Productions expressly produced animated TV ads and created the most remarkable commercial work of that period, climaxing in the so-called "Golden Age of Animated Commercials" (1957-59). Just about every ad of merit on TV at this time was a cartoon of some sort.

Even traditional products like Jell-O were given a fresh new appearance with animated commercials. General Foods had been promoting Jell-O, an American culinary staple, since the twenties with magazine ads that were often lofty ("The King and Queen will eat thereof/ And noblemen besides!"). They revitalized their product with a series of animated ads that celebrated non-events such as "Put the Bounce in the Baby Week," with a commercial showing a buoyant infant bouncing around his crib like a rubber ball, and "National Nutty Week" with an ad featuring a deranged stickman with an Ed Wynn-type voice. These commercials employed a sprightly jingle that admonished: "Tell everybody you know/ And don't, don't, don't let the week go by without J-E-L-L-O!"

Two Jell-O commercials remain the classics of this period, and both were written by Barbara Demaray of the Young & Rubicam agency.

"Prancing Boy" was drawn by Maurice Sendak in 1957. Sendak created a little boy who danced about a field of flowers, rode a pony made out of a Jell-O box, and sang the nonsense song, "Banana, manana, oh, I love banana..." Falling asleep in the tall grass, he dreamt of two new flavors: lemon and banana. Even the product-identification shot at the end was drawn in a loose, childlike style.

The charm of "Prancing Boy" was continued in the 1959 commercial "Chinese Baby." Ray Patin Productions animated Barbara Demaray's Y&R script, in which a Chinese-accented narrator intones: "Like to present ancient Chinese pantomime: 'Jell-O Tonight.'" A bamboo curtain rises on a "little Chinese-type baby" whose mother brings him "famous Western delicacy—Jell-O!" Unfortunately, the baby cannot eat his grape-flavored gelatin with his chopsticks; the stuff keeps slipping away. "Poor Chinese baby!" laments the narrator, "But, ah! Mother brings great Western invention—the spoon! Spoon was invented to eat Jell-O. Chinese baby velly happy!" The infant gobbles up the gelatin as the bamboo curtain descends once again. "So ends ancient Chinese pantomime," the narrator concludes. "Was pretty good commercial, no?"

Some of the most innovative commercials of the late fifties were automobile ads. Today, when auto ads consist mostly of MPG statistics, viewers might long for the days when Chevrolet

Maurice Sendak's "Prancing Boy" dances for Jell-O. The product's advertising was revitalized by a series of ambitious animated commercials with catchy jingles. (Young & Rubicam, 1957)

"Chinese Baby" takes delight in "a great Western delicacy—Jell-O!" The infant is frustrated because he cannot eat the slippery gelatin with his chopsticks. Jell-O's animated commercials were major award winners during the early years when commercial artistry was first being recognized. (Young & Rubicam, 1959)

took guileless delight in astounding the consumer with its commercials. Chevy seemed to say, "Look what we can do *this* year!" as it showed a man and a woman enjoying a ride along the highway *without a car*, which would belatedly materialize around them, or as it documented the reactions of pedestrians in Paris and New York while a flashy convertible drove by without a driver. They were fun, they were ingenuous, they surrounded the car with a very special aura, and they sold Chevies. A commercial can accomplish little more.

Campbell-Ewald, Chevrolet's agency, employed special effects extensively in its most memorable commercials, produced from the early to mid-sixties. For a time, agency and client would delight in topping themselves with ever more astonishing effects.

Back in the heady days when the new automotive model year was announced each October with the triumphal roar of a Second Coming, Chevrolet introduced its cars with epics of nearly Biblical proportions. In "Venice," a Christlike 1961 convertible drove on water atop a canal. Apotheosis was achieved by placing a '64 Chevy high atop a desert plateau in "Pinnacle." And in "Fusion," automotive parts flew out of the earth to assemble a '66 four-door, in the same way that Adam was molded from clay.

In 1963, Don Miller, for many years the head of production at Campbell-Ewald, hired engineer Bill Frick to place a '64 convertible on

A model waves from the front seat of a 1964 Chevrolet perched atop a pinnacle fifteen hundred feet above the desert floor. A helicopter airlifted the auto up in sections, and it was reassembled by an engineer who then hid beneath the car when the cameras rolled. (Campbell-Ewald, 1963)

top of a pinnacle fifteen hundred feet above the desert floor near Moab, Utah. The car was airlifted in sections by helicopter, and then daringly reassembled by the special effects engineer atop the plateau. The chopper then whirled around model Shirley Ramsey, who sat in the front seat waving cheerily. Frick kept the nervous actress company by hiding beneath the car. Pilots of commercial jets flying by that afternoon swamped air controllers with questions, wondering, as did millions of televiewers that autumn, how a car got up there. The image proved one of the most repeated in commercials, inspiring other ads that lofted electric razors, dog food, shampoo, and other products atop Monument Valley's plateaus, including a 1973 sedan in Chevrolet's own sequel, "Pinnacle Revisited."

An elaborate rig was constructed for "Fusion" to show the growth of a 1966 four-door. A grille flew out of the ocean. Four tires hanging on a tree bounced down and onto the axle. And so it went until the car stood fully assembled. Actually, the film sequence was shot in reverse. Invisible wires pulled the Chevy apart—the roof and doors first, the hood, engine, fenders, and seats next. Running the film backward made it appear as if the car magically grew from its components.

In "Split Car," engineer Frick sawed a 1967 Chevrolet in two so that viewers could glimpse the workings inside. Once the two halves had separated, they drove toward the camera and went their separate ways. Hidden wheels kept the pieces from collapsing. Shooting in the desert around Scottsdale, Arizona, the film crew needed a sloping road to assist the slow-moving car halves, which could only travel at fifteen miles an hour. A suitable road was located, but it turned out to be Senator Barry Goldwater's driveway. The Senator, a mechanical buff, was fascinated by the split car and supplied the crew with cold drinks throughout the shoot.

The witty Volkswagen commercials of the sixties not only created a national love affair with the ubiquitous, snub-nosed Beetle, but pioneered a self-deprecating style of ad that viewers found refreshing after so many years of inflated claims in rivals' advertising. The homely car whose style never changed at a time when American autos overhauled their looks each season, as fashions dictated, was seen as a gutsy little challenger. This perception was played up in a veritable hit parade of commercials created by the Doyle Dane Bernbach agency. "DDB happens to be the most creative agency of the 'greats,' " insists John Slaven, vice-president of advertising for Volkswagen of America. "We grew up with them. Since Volkswagen had a limited ad budget, we knew we would have to take chances and made a lot of noise."

Aired in 1963, "Snowplow" was DDB's breakthrough ad for Volkswagen. Over scenes of a Beetle chugging through a howling blizzard, an announcer asks, "Have you ever wondered how the man who drives a snowplow drives *to* the snowplow?" The Beetle then stops beside a snowbank. Its driver gets out and hops into the cab of a snowplow parked nearby, then begins to clear the same roadway the Beetle has just passed over. The announcer continues: "This one drives a Volkswagen. So you can stop wondering." The desolate arctic scene, captured in black and white, was filmed on Long Island at an incredibly low cost of $3,500. (Commercials today routinely cost anywhere from ten to one hundred times as much to produce, and often more.)

The "sameness" of the Beetle's styling was celebrated in an elaborate 1970 production titled " '49 Auto Show." According to Volkswagen's Slaven, "We felt the auto show was one of the most ridiculous exhibits of products in the United States. Their approach is, 'This year's model is the ultimate.' From that, the commercial wrote itself." In this commercial, the "ultimate models" of 1949 are displayed in all their chromium splendor in a meticulous period reconstruction. Postwar crowds ogle the DeSoto, the Kaiser, and a trio of Andrews Sisters lookalikes who warble, "Longer, lower, wider, the '49 Hudson is the car for you!" Meanwhile, a young man in a bow tie, who was being completely ignored, stands beside a Beetle, a car then newly introduced from Germany. He speaks to the air, since no one is listening. "We at Volkswagen don't believe in flashy design changes. But we do believe in making a car that will be around for a long time." Like other prophets, he and his message are lost in the confetti and the blare of swing bands promoting the automotive dinosaurs of yesteryear.

A Volkswagen Beetle braves a howling blizzard to deliver its driver to his snowplow, answering the question, "Did you ever wonder how the man who drives a snowplow drives *to* the snowplow?" The inexpensive but quirky ad was the first "hit" for Volkswagen from its agency, Doyle Dane Bernbach, a partnership that was to prove one of the most successful in advertising. (Doyle Dane Bernbach, 1963)

"Jones and Krempler" was a late-sixties spoof of suburbia and materialism, which were both under attack at the time. Two identical homes are shown side by side. A man drives his station wagon into the driveway on the left. "Mr. Jones and Mr. Krempler each had $3,000," an announcer informs us. "With his $3,000, Mr. Jones bought himself a brand-new car." Jones stands by his station wagon and watches a parade of deliverymen haul appliances into the house next door. "With *his* $3,000, Mr. Krempler bought a stereo, a dishwasher, a washing machine, a set of golf clubs, three new television sets, and a brand-new Volkswagen." Krempler parks his little red Beetle next to Jones's wagon, then waves to his neighbor as the announcer concludes: "Now Mr. Jones is faced with that age-old problem of keeping up with the Kremplers."

Economy was also the theme of "Funeral," written by DDB's Bob Levinson and directed by Howard Zieff, the same team that wrote "Jones and Krempler" and "'49 Auto Show." Zieff went on to direct such films as *Private Benjamin* and *Unfaithfully Yours.* "Funeral" opens with a procession of sleek black limousines. Inside each luxury car we see the "mourners" of a deceased multi-billionaire having a wonderful time thinking of the wealth that will be theirs after the reading of the will. But the deceased had other ideas. From beyond the grave, his

crotchety voice is heard reading his will: "To my wife, who spent money like there was no tomorrow, I leave one hundred dollars—and a calendar. To my sons, who spent every dime on fast cars and fast women, I leave one hundred dollars—in dimes. To my partner Jules, whose only motto is 'Spend, Spend, Spend!' I leave nothing, nothing, nothing! And to my nephew Harold . . ." A lone black Beetle rides at the tail end of the procession. Its driver, unlike the others, is genuinely moved. He wipes away a tear as we hear his uncle say, " . . . who ofttimes said, 'A penny saved is a penny earned,' and who also ofttimes said, 'Gee, Uncle Max, it sure pays to drive a Volkswagen!' I leave my entire fortune—of one hundred billion dollars."

This happy parable climaxed Volkswagen's TV commercial hit parade. A few years later the company stopped manufacturing the lovable Beetle. No other car has quite engendered the affection of this model, and it was the Beetle's eccentric, almost human personality that gave DDB a solid foundation on which to craft its witty commercials.

Every decade seems to have its popular illustrator who manages to capture the spirit of his times in his work, and, in turn, establishes the "look" of the times. The Gibson Girl defined turn-of-the-century America the way John Held, Jr.'s flappers defined the Roaring Twenties. Vargas's pin-up girls captured the forties, and Peter Max with his psychedelic mindscapes illuminated the sixties. Appropriately, the "look" of the computerized seventies and eighties originated in the computer-generated animated graphics of television commercials; in particular the flashy, fiery neonesque images floating against black space that became the trademark of Robert Abel.

After laboring in obscurity for years, animating logos for ABC television, Robert Abel and Associates' Hollywood studio became the hottest production house in town with its 1974 Seven-Up commercial "Bubbles." In this survey of thirty years' worth of American pop music, viewers swam through the carbonated drink and watched winged fantasy females trail glitter like Tinker Bell's fairy dust. The ad's "Candy Apple Neon" effect was inspired by the "kinetic art" that Abel admired as a Southern California youth in the fifties, especially George Barris's flashy customized cars and the enameled designs that decorated the surfboards Abel rode over the waves of Santa Monica Bay. The "outlaw" graphics of the fifties' hot rods became the respected corporate look two decades later, when Abel animated logos for General

A fantasy female flies through an animated dreamscape for Seven-Up. Nothing quite like this dazzling commercial, with its computer-generated graphics, had been seen before by televiewers. It established the reputation of Robert Abel, whose neonesque images established the contemporary "look" of the seventies. (N. W. Ayer, 1974)

Motors, Kodak, TWA, RCA, and dozens of other firms.

Abel's out-of-this-world animation can often be compared to an alien landscape: spectacular, brilliant, and new, but also cold and inhuman. His most daring ad, however, was also one of his most exhilarating, a Kawasaki commercial titled "The Ultimate Trip." This ad attempts to duplicate the experience of riding a motorcycle—"the freedom, the distorted perspective as things rush up at you, the 'streaking' effect as scenery flashes by, glowing, going into the vortex," according to Kawasaki's agency, J. Walter Thompson. This summation is also a description of a psychedelic experience induced by hallucinogenic drugs, especially the "streaking" effect. The commercial's title, "The Ultimate Trip," was also the advertising copy line for *2001: A Space Odyssey,* and the Kawasaki ad is a simulation of the "psychedelic trip"

that ended Stanley Kubrick's film. After an initial soft-focus shot of U.S. speedway champion Mike Bust riding a Kawasaki, the ad cuts to a close-up of Bust behind his helmet's transparent face mask, like the spaceman in *2001.* Then, as in the movie, we experience the passing scenery from his point of view. Green trees turn orange, the sky green. The gray asphalt road becomes a brilliant yellow ribbon. Balls of white fire roar by as the soundtrack's music distorts to an electronic din. Color, lights, and sound crescendo until we "black out." Rows of animated motorcycles appear as the announcer says with a hint of friendly intimacy: "Kawasaki. We *know* why you ride!"

This 1977 commercial is the only known ad to be censored by the networks for being "antisocial" and for allegedly "inducing people to take drugs." The networks initially approved the commercial, but then an executive at

Hallucinogenic scenery flashes by in Kawasaki's "Ultimate Trip." The view seen by the motorcyclist was reminiscent of the climactic psychedelic "trip" from the movie *2001: A Space Odyssey.* Both ABC and CBS censored the commercial for allegedly "contributing to the use of drugs by motorcyclists." (J. Walter Thompson, 1977)

Levi's "pet" trademark is freed from its leash by a Forty-niner prospecting the wash from a fireplug. As fantastic as a dream, the commercial, which follows the trademark's adventures up a magical sidewalk, was accomplished using a marionette, stylized acting, a new computerized film camera, and incredible animation. (Foote, Cone & Belding, 1977)

ABC's department of standards and practices took a look, became alarmed by what he saw, and phoned a colleague at CBS. Off went the commercial, but not before viewers had made it a cult classic, one they could still see on imperturable, or merely inattentive, NBC.

The Kawasaki troubles aside, 1977 was an important year for Robert Abel and Associates; the year that also saw the production of the landmark Levi Strauss commercial, "Brand Name." "Combining technology with creative fantasy is the hallmark of our work," says Abel. For the story of a "pet" Levi's trademark that breaks away from its master's leash and frolics up a magical sidewalk peopled by models in

Levi's fashions, a prototype computer-controlled camera was invented. The little trademark—a marionette designed by Bob Baker of the Muppets, who later built E.T.—and its surreal journey were conceived by Mike Koelker of the Foote, Cone & Belding agency. Koelker's guiding philosophy is an "absolute determination to put on television something that nobody has seen before." His concept of what he calls "strategically altered reality" was evident in the 1971 commercials "Evolution" and "The Stranger," both of which established the look of Levi's acclaimed ads of the seventies. Directed by John Urie, the man whom Bob Abel unabashedly calls "a genius who probably started more people and trends in Hollywood than any other ten people," "The Stranger" shows a mysterious man who walks down the main street of a small town and zaps its gray-clad citizens with his finger, turning their monochromatic clothes into bright Levi's styles. Or, as John Urie himself says, "Oh my God! This man just came by and changed my pants!" Urie filmed actors pantomiming the scenes, then had animators paint over their photographed images so "they were not quite people and not quite cartoons," a technique that was later used extensively in theatrical animated films.

Viewers marveled at how "The Stranger"

Levi's "The Stranger" comes to town. With a flick of his finger he changes the monochromatic pants of a town's male inhabitants to garish colors popular in the early seventies. A technique called "rotoscoping" was employed to make the ad's characters look "not quite like humans, not quite like cartoons." (Foote, Cone & Belding, 1971)

was done, just as they would wonder at the sights seen by the wandering trademark six years later. One thing on which sponsors, agencies, and production companies all agree is that no commercial sets out to be "artsy" for art's sake, or tries to startle and impress when the earnest business of selling products is paramount. Once stated, though, these assertions are best forgotten, because too many filmic innovations are pioneered in commercials, and too much fun and love of craft permeates these miniature productions to disguise the true spirit of their makers.

The tension between the businessman's needs and the filmmaker's art is the dynamic

that makes the television commercial a unique pop-art form. Consider Alka-Seltzer. This product of Miles Laboratories was responsible for some of the most entertaining commercials ever broadcast. Alka-Seltzer commercials inspired a hit song and a dance craze. They have won every advertising award. Phrases like "Try it, you'll like it!" and the doleful "I can't believe I ate the whole thing!" from its 1972 campaign entered the national lexicon. Viewers foolish enough to talk during the Alka-Seltzer ads were politely but firmly told to shut up. These were the Great Commercials.

But when asked the importance of entertainment and innovation in commercials, a

A diner cheerfully suggests, "Try it, you'll like it!" He later regrets his advice and takes Alka-Seltzer. This commercial introduced one of advertising's most repeated copy lines. (Wells, Rich & Greene, 1972)

A man makes a point on his companion's stomach in "Tummies." The instrumental music from this commercial, which shows a montage of stomachs of every shape and size, was recorded by the T-Bones as "No Matter What Shape Your Stomach's In." The recording became a Top Ten hit, and eventually went "gold," selling over a million copies. It was not long before discotheques rocked with a new dance called "The Poke," inspired by the opening scene of the Alka-Seltzer commercial above. (Jack Tinker & Partners, 1965)

Miles Laboratories spokesman voices the same sentiments expressed by virtually all advertisers: "Advertising is a communications task resulting in a motivation to buy. If Miles can utilize humor in sparking that motivation, this is fine, but getting our message across is our major aim in communicating with the viewers."

One suspects that if advertisers could get away with waving a sign before the camera that orders viewers to "BUY!" they would be satisfied. Fortunately, viewers are not so easily satisfied. They demand to be entertained by a good jingle, a memorable sentiment, a witty line. It takes all the conjuring skill of a movie magician to break through the clutter of competing tele-

vision commercials. And it is with this conjuring act that Alka-Seltzer and its agencies have enjoyed considerable success.

When Speedy Alka-Seltzer went on his extended vacation in 1964, Jack Tinker and Partners, Miles's agency at the time, hired director Howard Zieff to shoot a variety of human stomachs on their painful way to cases of heartburn. Titled "Tummies," the resulting ad created a national sensation. Against a harmonica, guitar, and organ instrumental piece (performed by the pop group the T-Bones), a prizefighter's stomach is pummeled by left jabs, a go-go dancer's stomach gyrates, a hardhat's pot belly bounces against a jackhammer, and a business-

Another popular theme line from an Alka-Seltzer ad that found its way into general usage was this indigestion victim's lament: "I can't believe I ate the whole thing." His unsympathetic wife later asks if he swallowed his Alka-Seltzer as she advised. Beaming, he replies, "The whole thing!" (Wells, Rich, Greene, 1972)

man's silhouetted paunch is repeatedly poked by a companion gesturing with his finger to make a point.

A tummy was also the star of R. O. Blechman's 1971 cartoon commercial "Man vs. Stomach." Using his signature "squiggly line" drawing style, Blechman created an anthropomorphic stomach that hotly berates its bland male owner over the exotic food it is forced to digest. "You should see the way he *stuffs* himself at his mother's!" the stomach complains. Then, attacking his "master" again: "And the pepperoni pizzas!"

"I *like* pepperoni pizza!" the man answers.

"Do you like heartburn? Well, you're going

In "Man vs. Stomach," a bilious battle is settled by Alka-Seltzer. A man guilty of indulging in stomach-churning foods is forced to confront his offended organ. (Jack Tinker & Partners, 1971)

to get it!" the stomach shouts, raising its fists and threatening the man. An announcer begs for peace, citing the curative power of Alka-Seltzer, and leaves the two antagonists moodily

George Raft plays one of his hard-boiled cons in Alka-Seltzer's spoof of prison movies titled "The Unfinished Lunch."

agreeing to try and get along.

"The Unfinished Lunch" was the ironic title given to a 1969 prison-movie spoof starring George Raft. TV commercial director Lee Lacey re-created the look and feel of a penitentiary dining hall. Disgusted by the inedible food, Raft throws down his fork, grabs his tin cup, and begins to pound the table. The other prisoners do the same. Thus far, the viewer hasn't a clue as to what this drama is about. Raft, his face red with fury, begins to chant, "Alka-Seltzer! Alka-Seltzer!" The cons at his table pick up the refrain, then the convicts surrounding them, until the dining hall resounds with the rhythmic chant of a thousand angry men: "ALKA-SELTZER! ALKA-SELTZER!" A little miracle of directing, acting, and writing, the ad ends with the name of the product superimposed over the tumultuous prison scene.

The prisoners' revolt crescendoes as the cry arises from a thousand throats: "ALKA-SELTZER! ALKA-SELTZER!" (Jack Tinker & Partners, 1970)

It was perhaps inevitable that Alka-Seltzer became the client of the innovative Doyle Dane Bernbach agency during 1969-70, the "Golden Age of Television Commercials." Even in this remarkably creative time, a pair of Alka-Seltzer ads stood out. In "Groom's First Meal," a bride lies on the bed of a honeymoon suite, glorying in the success of her first home-cooked meal. Meanwhile, she thumbs through a cookbook,

A bride torments her husband with stomach-wrenching recipes in "The Groom's First Meal," another of Alka-Seltzer's hit comedies from the Golden Age of television commercials, approximately 1969–70. (Doyle Dane Bernbach, 1970)

plotting future exotic fare. The groom silently suffers from heartburn in the background. "That meal really sticks to your ribs, doesn't it?" the bride giggles.

"That's just where it stuck," her husband says glumly.

"What, dear?"

"Oh, nothing!" the man insists with forced cheerfulness. "It's just that I've never seen a dumpling that big before!"

"Oh, I thought it would be nicer than a lot of little ones!" the wife says, pleased with herself. At the bathroom sink, the man drops two Alka-Seltzer tablets into a glass of water. Hearing the fizz, his bride asks, "Is it raining, dear?"

The man covers the noisy glass, gulps its contents, then bravely rejoins his wife and her cookbook. "Next time—poached oysters!" she chirps. The groom pivots without breaking stride and returns immediately to the bathroom. Fade-out.

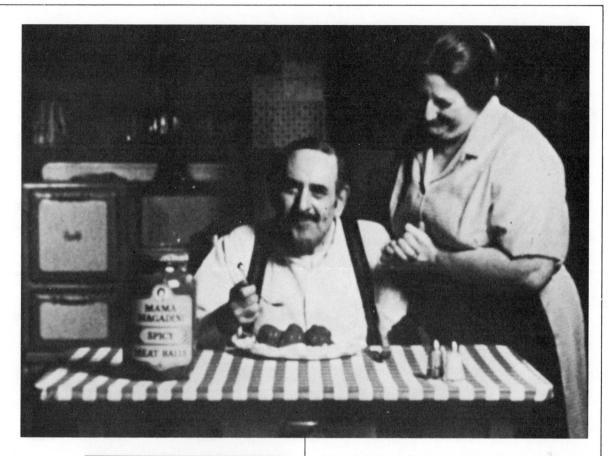

Jack, the TV commercial actor, proclaimed "Mama mia, that's a spicey meat-a ball!" In this commercial-within-a-commercial, perhaps the most popular video ad of all time, the actor flubbed his lines or was plagued by production snafus until the fictitious sponsor's product gave him heartburn. He was cured, of course, by the *real* sponsor's product, Alka-Seltzer. (Doyle Dane Bernbach, 1970)

Just as everyone could sympathize with the plight of the hapless groom, so too did viewers identify with the frustrations of "Jack," the actor who continually blew his lines in "Magdanini's Meatballs," one of the most popular commercials of all time.

To many fans of TV commercials, who believe that these finely crafted minute movies are often superior to the programs they allegedly "interrupt," "Magdanini's Meatballs" represents the zenith of commercial making. It has everything a good commercial must have: wit, elegance of acting and direction (again by Howard Zieff), and the ability to memorably communciate a product's identity and what that product does, with a minimum of hard sell.

It is unfair to expect even the so-called "classic" commercials to bear up under the scrutiny that is a routine part of the criticism of the fine arts. If TV commercials are a form of popular art, they are art by default. Businesses are out to sell products. If their advertisements are good, like the ones highlighted in this volume, fine. Commercials are a unique pop cultural genre precisely because they manage to enthrall with music, dance, humor, and drama, even while the products they celebrate may be proved unhealthful, unsafe, or simply worthless. A new pop art springs like a fountain from the compost heap of American consumer products. It is alchemical.

Chapter Seven

Jingles
and
Sentimentality

"We Good to

Often a jingle will be the most memorable element of a commercial. Knowing that a snappy tune will implant a sponsor's product firmly in the consumer's mind, advertisers often design their commercials around a jingle or an instrumental "hook."

In the "Go, Go, Goodyear" ads of the early sixties, mu-

146

bring Things Life!"

sic and picture were blended to create a Hitchcock-type "montage," the juxtaposing of images to create a certain psychological effect. The Young & Rubicam agency's account executive for Goodyear, Hanley Norins, conceived the campaign. Norins had begun writing commercial jingles for radio in the forties. As a lyricist, he had collaborated with a classical violinist named Jack Atherton, son of the president of the Boston ad agency Atherton & Courier. With Norins writing the lyrics and Atherton composing the music, the duo created the 1946 commercial hit, "Brylcreem, a Little Dab Will Do Ya." Norins went on to create entire commercial campaigns during the fifties. His favorite was a live demonstration commercial on *What's My Line?* in 1953, in which a Remington electric razor shaved first the fuzz from a peach, then the bristles from a brush.

Heading up the Goodyear account at Y&R in 1961, Norins collaborated with composer

Bob Thompson on "Go, Go, Goodyear." "I think the most successful TV jingles have been very innovative visually," Norins says. This is particularly true with the Goodyear snow tire ads that were inspired by the theatrical "coming attractions" promotional film for *La Dolce Vita*, seen in movie houses in 1961. "I admired the quick cutting used for that trailer, and I wanted to get the same rhythmic effect. There was no dialogue at all in the commercial, just stock footage of cars stuck in the snow." A single-word title appeared on the screen with each musical beat: "WHEN...SNOW...SAYS... NO...GOODYEAR...SAYS...GO!" With

the concluding shot of a car speeding through the blizzard on Goodyear snow tires, the upbeat "Go, Go, Goodyear" theme played. A skillful combination of music and visuals made this a striking and memorable commercial for one of the least glamorous products to advertise.

"Any good piece of music will take hold after a long period of time," says Charles Foll, president of Vantage Advertising, whose client, the Golden Grain Macaroni Company of San Leandro, California, has had twenty years to establish its jingle for Rice-A-Roni, "The San Francisco Treat." In 1961, when both Foll and Golden Grain were with the McCann-Erickson agency, Rice-A-Roni was about to break out of the San Francisco market, where it had become a local culinary tradition, and achieve national distribution. "Rather than use a *hu-*

A cable car chugs up a hill bearing a Rice-A-Roni poster announcing "the San Francisco Treat." This image was reinforced by the sponsors until even the city's cable cars became identifiable characters for the product. (McCann-Erickson, 1961)

man spokesman," recalls Foll, "we decided to use our city, specifically the cable cars that are an integral part of its charm. At the time, San Francisco was getting a lot of press as the 'jewel city.' And since it's also noted as a good-eating city, that was also in our favor."

"The San Francisco Treat" jingle began as a woodblock instrumental in 1958. Its melody is an inversion of "Barney Google," the popular song of the twenties. Lyrics were added for Rice-A-Roni's first national TV commercial in 1961:

Rice-A-Roni, the San Francisco treat
Rice-A-Roni, the flavor can't be beat
One pan, no boiling, cooking ease
A flavor that is sure to please
Rice-A-Roni, the San Francisco treat!

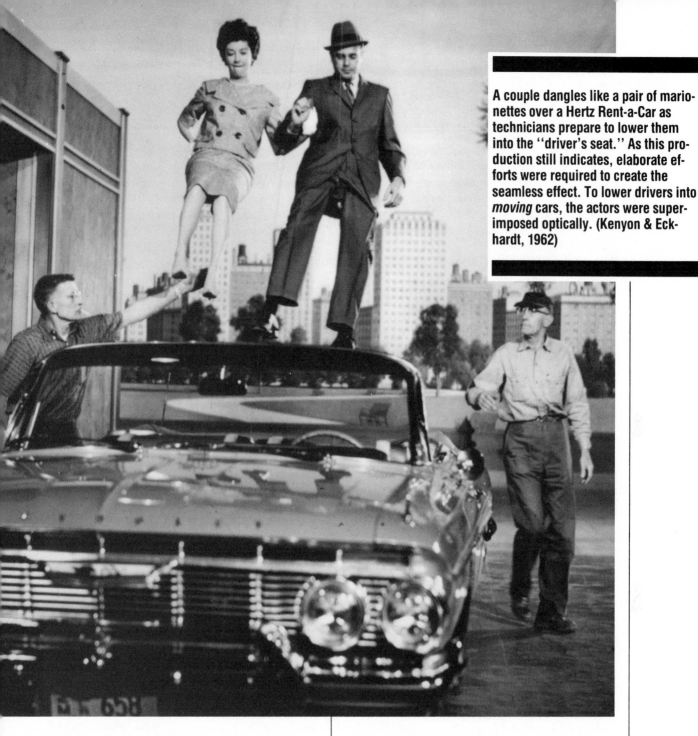

The song played against scenes of the Golden Gate Bridge, and was punctuated by the clanging bell of a cable car lumbering up a hill on Powell Street, with Alcatraz Island in the background. This scene has been featured in virtually all Rice-A-Roni commercials for more than twenty years.

One of the most fantastic and arresting visuals ever seen in commercials, combined with one of advertising's most singable jingles, made the "Let Hertz Put You in the Driver's Seat" series a true classic. To symbolize the swiftness of renting an automobile from Hertz, these ads of the early sixties showed men, women, couples,

and entire families flying through the air in a sitting position until they were gradually lowered into a convertible car that, propelled along by its own magic, sped over the highway driverless. It was the kind of startling nonsense seen only in television commercials. The ad, a creation of the Kenyon & Eckhardt agency, was so popular it was spoofed in the 1964 movie *Good Neighbor Sam*, featuring Jack Lemmon as a favorite literary stereotype, the tormented advertising executive. The film's running gag had a hapless actor dropped again and again into a car, crashing through the convertible's cloth roof or missing the car entirely and landing on the pavement. In the actual Hertz television commercials, various methods were employed to lower passengers into cars, from invisible wires to superimposition. But as they made their descent, by whatever special-effects technique, a male chorus would always sing the tuneful Hertz jingle:

Let Hertz put you in the driver's seat
Let Hertz take you anywhere at all
At work
At play
At home
Away
Let Hertz put you in the driver's seat today
Let Hertz put you in the driver's seat
Let Hertz take you anywhere at all
By the hour
By the day
By the week
Or any way
Just let Hertz put you in the driver's seat
Today!

The final "you" was elongated as the driver eased in behind the steering wheel.

"The rent-a-car business was *built* on advertising," reports Murray Gaylord, account executive at Scali, McCabe and Slaves, Hertz's current agency. "Prior to the 'Driver's Seat' campaign, only one percent of the country rented cars. Renters were wealthy. It was a 'class, not mass' business." But the sight of drivers gliding into moving cars in the first rent-a-car commercials to be aired nationally made consumers aware of the new service. Hertz soon grabbed 70 percent of the market, which is today up to 10 percent of the population, although the company has since lost some of its market share to rivals, and especially to the feisty Avis, promoted by Doyle Dane Bernbach's "We Try Harder" campaign, and National, whose commercials showed comedian Don Rickles pacified by that company's service.

In 1974, several years after the flying drivers had been grounded, Ted Bates, Hertz's agency at the time, hired football superstar O.J. Simpson as company spokesman. Simpson still holds the NFL record for yardage gained during a game, and acts regularly in films and on television. He became the third-most-recognizable personality in commercials. In his first Hertz ads, Simpson, attired in a three-piece suit, ran through airport terminals, jumping over suitcases, personifying the speed of renting a car from Hertz, "the Superstar in Rent-a-Car," as he claimed. But when Hertz introduced its Express Service in 1979, which made it easier to rent a car at an airport, an advertising dilemma occurred. According to Murray Gaylord, "We had had O.J. Simpson running through an airport already, so how do we communicate the additional speed? He'd *fly* through airports."

Backgrounds were shot at the newly completed United Terminal at San Francisco International Airport. These were combined with shots of Simpson "flying," which had been created at the Walt Disney Studios in Burbank, California, by the same special-effects men who levitated Christopher Reeve in *Superman*. In the final shot of the commercial, O.J. was lowered through a car's sun roof, a return to the very first "Let Hertz Put You in the Driver's Seat" ads. The final word, though, belonged to Reggie Rucker of the Cleveland Browns, who looked at the commercial and asked, "If this guy can fly, why does he need to rent a car?"

The Oscar Mayer company also has a way with jingles. Little Andy Lambros first sang his "My Bologna Has a First Name" jingle in the 1975 commercial "Fisherman." This commercial is still on the air today. "My bologna has a first name, it's O-S-C-A-R," sings the curly-haired little boy sitting on a pier, tugging at his red toy fishing pole with one hand while nursing a huge sandwich in the other. "My bologna has a second name, it's M-A-Y-E-R/Oh! I love to eat it every day, and if you ask me why, I'll say"—his voice cracks on the high note, and he giggles—" 'cause Oscar Mayer has a way with B-O-L-O-G-N-A!"

But put in perspective, this commercial is a continuation of the success with jingles enjoyed over the years by Oscar Mayer, the Madison, Wisconsin-based cold cut and hot dog maker. Introduced in a 1963 radio spot, and in 1965 in an animated television commercial, was this memorable ditty:

Oh, I'd love to be an Oscar Mayer wiener
That is what I'd truly like to be
'Cause if I were an Oscar Mayer wiener
Ev'ryone would be in love with me!

SCALI, McCABE, SLOVES, INC.
CLIENT: HERTZ CORPORATION
PRODUCT: RENT-A-CAR

TITLE: "O.J. SOLO"
LENGTH: 30 SECONDS
COMM'L. NO.:   RCHC 0503

1. O.J.: I used to run through airports.

2. Now I fly! Through them

3. (MUSIC)

4. With new Hertz #1 Express service....

5. I fly nonstop...
...from my plane to my car.

6. Without stopping at the counter.

7. If you ask for #1 Express when you make a reservation

8. your Ford or other fine car and contract will be waiting at the

9. #1 Express booth.

10. (MAN'S REACTION)

11. Once again, Hertz puts you in...

12. ...the driver's seat...
...faster than anybody else.

TED BATES ADVERTISING, 1979

Andy Lambros tells us, "My bologna has a first name, it's O-S-C-A-R!" He became the most popular spokeschild since Mikey, with his giggly rendition of Oscar Mayer's popular jingle. (J. Walter Thompson, 1975)

"Oh, I wish I were an Oscar Mayer Wiener . . ." A boy applauds the Vienna Symphony Orchestra for their performance of the Oscar Mayer "Wiener Song." In this "classical" adaptation, the lyrics were superimposed over the furiously performing violins and the maestro's dramatic gestures. (J. Walter Thompson, 1968)

The "Wiener Song" was one of those inescapable tunes that, once heard, would obsess listeners throughout the day. One tormented woman from Fox River Grove, Illinois, wrote to Oscar Mayer's agency, J. Walter Thompson, requesting a recording of the jingle. "I figure if I just let it run over and over on my hi-fi, then it will have a curative effect on my subconscious and I may get over this mental madness of forever thinking the tune."

But for this woman and others, relief would not come soon. Buoyed by the success of its first "Wiener Song" commercial, Oscar Mayer traveled next to Europe to film the Vienna Symphony Orchestra performing the tune. With a verve they might lavish on Beethoven, the orchestra played while the jingle lyrics were superimposed over the bottom of the picture. When they finished, a lone boy, the only listener in the baroque concert hall, clapped his hands, then took a bite from his hot dog. Intoned the announcer: "The Oscar Mayer wiener: a classic."

Coca-Cola, the most familiar consumer product in the world, dramatized its international appeal and simultaneously launched a hit song with a commercial that was first aired during the summer of 1971, "Buy the World." The McCann-Erickson agency assembled a group of teenage Coke drinkers from six continents on a hilltop outside London. But British rains washed out the production, and the group was relocated to another, sunnier hilltop outside Rome. As each held a Coke bottle labeled in the language of his or her native country, they sang:

I'd like to buy the world a home
And furnish it with love
Grow apple trees and honeybees
And snow-white turtledoves
I'd like to teach the world to sing
In perfect harmony
I'd like to buy the world a Coke
And keep it company
It's the Real Thing, Coke is
What the world wants today
It's the Real Thing.

The simple but impressive ad, with its message of brotherhood, prompted five thousand congratulatory letters to flood Coke's headquarters in Atlanta. The company began sending out sheet music and 45 rpm recordings of the jingle performed by the New Seekers. Another group, the Hillside Singers, cut a record as well, and both versions, with references to Coca-Cola deleted so that radio stations would not consider them three-minute commercials, became Top Forty hits by Christmas. By that time, Coke's Yuletide ad, "Christmas Tree," was on the air. In this commercial, an illuminated star is seen in close-up atop a giant Douglas fir. The camera pulls back while strings of lights switch on to the beat of the music, gradually outlining the massive tree. Carolers cluster around the tree to sing the now-familiar jingle.

In 1977, both versions of the ad were combined in "Candles." A new and enthusiastic international collection of young people is seen reassembled on the Italian hilltop. From the air they form a large Christmas tree, their candles flickering in the twilight as they sing. Coca-Cola's new Christmas carol, still shown every year, inspired another outpouring of mail. Grade-school children composed their own lyrics and sent them to Coke. Other viewers requested that the commercial be aired beyond Christmas. And one savvy youngster wrote: "Dear Coke: I have heard in your ads that you would like to buy the whole world a Coke. Well, I don't know about the rest of the world, but as for me, you can buy me a Coke. You may send the money to Kevin Michel, Lawrence, Kansas."

In contrast with the large-scale soda pop musical productions, the tuneful vignettes of C and H Sugar seemed as delicate as a daydream. They were no less effective, and their charm proved widespread. Each ad chronicled the adventures of Hawaiian children among the sugar-cane fields of Maui. "In Hawaii, our children grow up with the sugar cane," narrated the singer, who then rendered a jingle whose melody was borrowed from "Pearly Shells." A chorus of children repeated each line he sang: "C and H/Pure cane sugar/From Hawaii/Growing in the sun/Island sugar, growing pure, fresh and clean/C and H pure cane sugar is the one."

Of the series, the most endearing vignette

Coca-Cola's ode to brotherhood, "I'd Like to Teach the World to Sing," became a Top Forty hit. (McCann-Erickson, 1977)

An international collection of young people sing out for Coca-Cola and world peace, in that order, as they gather on an Italian hillside. This remake of a 1971 original became Coke's Christmas commercial, and it inspired an outpouring of fan mail and requests for song lyrics. (McCann-Erickson, 1977)

On a hilltop in Italy,
We assembled young people
From all over the world...
To bring you this message
From Coca-Cola Bottlers
All over the world.
It's the real thing. Coke.

was a 1974 ad titled "Kimo's Cane." While the jingle plays, Kimo is seen planting a baby sugar-cane stalk in the ruddy Maui soil. Having identified his patch of earth with a hand-painted sign, "Kimo's Cane," he runs off to find his friends. By the time they return, Kimo's grandfather, who has watched the child's diligent work, has substituted a full-grown sugar cane for the sprout, leaving an awed Kimo staring up at the miraculous growth in one of commercials' greatest "takes." The ad leaves Kimo in his island paradise, trying to convince his companions of the miracle.

Ever since a former employee, Kurt Vonnegut, Jr., penned the slogan, "At General Elec-

tric, Progress Is Our Most Important Product," the giant appliance and electronics firm had been looking for a central theme to unite its diversified products. With its 1979 commercial jingle, "We Bring Good Things to Life," GE not only discovered its own corporate identity, but graphically reminded viewers how a major firm and its technology has integrated itself into the bones and marrow of daily American life.

GE's agency, BBD&O, hired jingle writer Lucas McFaul to come up with the lyrics: "We bring new friends to play/We wake you to the sun/We bake your bread/Light your way/When day is done..." Quick vignettes, meanwhile, show a pair of small girls practicing their

C and H SUGAR
Two of the
1974 Television Commercials

imo's Cane :30

EAD SINGER: (Spoken) In awaii . . . our children grow p with the sugar cane.

SINGS: ("Pearly Shells") C and H
KIDS: C and H

LEAD: Pure cane sugar
KIDS: Pure cane sugar

LEAD: From Hawaii
KIDS: From Hawaii

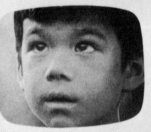

LEAD: Growing in the sun
KIDS: Growing in the sun

ALL: Island sugar

Growing pure fresh and clean

C and H pure cane sugar is the one.

Treehouse :30

LEAD SINGER: (Spoken) In Hawaii . . . our children grow up with the sugar cane.

SINGS: ("Pearly Shells") C and H
KIDS: C and H

LEAD: Pure cane sugar
KIDS: Pure cane sugar

LEAD: From Hawaii
KIDS: From Hawaii

LEAD: Growing in the sun
KIDS: Growing in the sun

ALL: Island sugar

Growing pure fresh and clean

C and H pure cane sugar is the one.

BBDO

Batten, Barton, Durstine & Osborn, Inc.

Client: **GENERAL ELECTRIC** Time: **60 SECONDS**

Product: **CONSUMER BRAND** Title: **"WE BRING GOOD THINGS TO LIFE" I** Comml. No.: **GECS 9016**

SINGERS: We make your daughters dance

SINGERS: Wake you to the sun

SINGERS: We bake you bread

SINGERS: Light your way when day is done

SINGERS: We make you pretty

SINGERS: We make you smile

SINGERS: GE

SINGERS: We bring good things to living

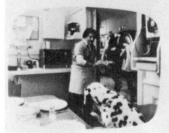
SINGERS: We bring good things to life

ANNCR: (VO) At GE we're in the business of making products that make your life a little easier.

A little better. And you know something?

That's a pretty nice business to be in.

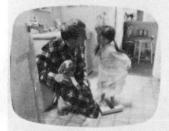
SINGERS: We bring you closer

to the ones you love.

SINGERS: GE

SINGERS: We bring good things to living

SINGERS: GE

SINGERS: We bring good things to life

SINGERS: GE

SINGERS: We bring good things to living
We bring good things to life.

ballet lessons by the stereo, a sleepy student turning off his alarm radio, an elderly couple pulling biscuits from the oven, and a toddler guided to his bedroom by a hallway night light. In other scenes, a mother tumble-dries her infant's teddy bear, a boy practices his trombone, inspired by a marching band he sees on his TV, a father videotapes his daughter's first ride on a carousel, and rollerskaters boogie up the sidewalk, shouldering weighty radios. All the while, viewers are reminded, "We bring you closer to the ones you love/GE, we bring good things to living"—and, yes, though these tech-nological gadgets may be taken for granted, the ads demonstrated how they have become the essentials of our life-styles—"we bring good things to life!"

Sentimental appeals and ditties are but two effective ways for advertisers to seduce the consumer. By using aspects of popular culture in advertising, sponsors have, in turn, created a new form of popular culture in commercials, a symbiotic relationship between pop art and commerce which has always been the elemental reason for any classic commercial's appeal and success.

Dr. Ellis's little girl grows up in Ko-dak's commercial "Turn Around." This series began with this award-winning portrait, "Left Behind." (J. Walter Thompson, 1961)

Seventeen years later, Judy models her high school prom dress. (J. Walter Thompson, 1961)

"Turn Around" ends with Judy, now grown and married, posing with her own child, Jeffrey. The cycle of life continues. Not only did the girl from California come of age during Kodak's remarkable two-minute ad, but so did the television commercial as a genre of American popular art. (J. Walter Thompson, 1961)

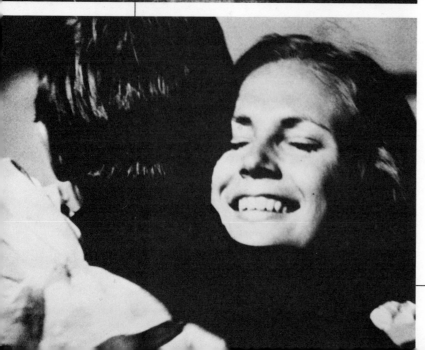

SOME FROM THE HEART

On April 16, 1961, Ed Sullivan announced to his viewers, "And now I'd like to present the most interesting pictures we've ever had on our program." What followed was an Eastman Kodak commercial titled "Turn Around." Two minutes later, when it was over, there were few dry eyes among Sullivan's millions of viewers. What America saw that Sunday evening was a commercial that elevated the medium to the status of a popular art form. Kodak's commercial was sentimental, as many commercials are. But this ad featured sentiment with a difference; it was honest, documenting a real life, and was not based on some copywriter's contrivance.

The song "Turn Around" was sung by a gentle-voiced man over a series of photographs showing a massive oaken door that acted as a backdrop to the life of a little girl. She is first seen as an infant, her bare bottom toward the camera as she strains to push open the unyielding door:

Where are you going my little one?
Where are you going, my baby, my own?

Year by year, we watch the girl grow up as she poses before the door in her best dresses:

Turn around and you're two
Turn around and you're four
Turn around and you're a young
girl going out of the door...

She is now a teenager, modeling her dress for the high school prom.

Turn around and you're a young wife,
with babes of your own...

Now a married woman, she stands not against the familiar old door, but in the nursery of her new home, cradling her baby boy. The cycle of life continues.

The man who took the pictures, Dr. Irving Ellis of Piedmont, California, was not a casual photographer. The commercial's opening image of his daughter, Judy, as a naked infant before the oak door was an award-winning photograph titled "Left Behind" that had earned Ellis a 1941 Packard Clipper automobile in a contest sponsored by *Popular Photography*. But when Ellis sent Judy's pictures to Kodak, J. Walter Thompson, Kodak's agency, saw them as a dramatic way to demonstrate to parents how they, too, might preserve their child's young life on film. To round out the sequence of pictures, they took one final shot of the woman, now Judy Glickman, with her own baby, Jeffrey. The choice of music and skillful editing also heightened the emotional impact. From that point on, sentimental commercials became the thrust of Kodak's advertising.

With its two-minute-long commercials, Kodak had the luxury of time needed to unfold its mini-dramas, aired during special events like the Academy Awards ceremony, which the company sponsored every spring. Kodak often rivaled the motion pictures that were up for Oscars with beautiful small-screen stories like 1970's "Green Grass." Inspired by a popular country song, "Green Grass" follows a young veteran back from the Vietnam War as he returns to his rural town. A joyous reunion begins at the bus stop with an embrace from his girl, Mary, her "hair of gold and lips like cherries," and climaxes with a family picnic at the farmhouse, where an aunt busily snaps pictures with her Instamatic. As in "Turn Around," a male singer tells the story. No dialogue is needed as the young man greets old friends, inspects the house, and finally concludes, "It's good to feel the green, green grass of home."

The little town of Storm Lake, Iowa, was recruited to star in the commercial. No professional actors were used; the young man was an actual army vet, and "Mary" was his real wife. In the commercial he returns to his parents' home, and the relatives shown were the same familiar faces he had known all his life. Viewers sensed this authenticity, but, more important, they were moved by the commercial's sentiment. In 1970, America wanted to rid itself of the continuing trauma of Vietnam, to catch its breath after years of violent turmoil at home, to

rediscover its roots and the enduring values of family and the land. And it was a television commercial, "Green Grass," that best exemplified this feeling.

That memories, as well as life itself, can be preserved on film for all time was the theme of Polaroid's most endearing commercial, "Zoo," produced in 1963. Cameraman/director Michael Nebbia, who, according to a colleague, "uses his camera like a violin, floating it through the air and letting it sing," brought to life the script created by Phillis Robinson and Bob Gage of the Doyle Dane Bernbach agency. The ad was a simple story about a young father and his five-year-old daughter spending a Sunday afternoon at the Central Park Zoo. They see the animals, wander past the cages while a nostalgic and evocative musical score by Mitch Leigh plays, and take a ride in a hansom cab, where the father looks at the Polaroid photos he has taken of the little girl, who is now asleep in his lap. The announcer's single line sums it up: "If you don't have a Polaroid camera, there's something left out of your life."

Stanley Grover and his daughter Cindy starred in the ad. Grover, his wife, and three children had all acted in previous TV commercials, and once appeared together as a clan in a Clairol commercial. But it is Cindy's story that provides some interesting insights into the life of a TV commercial prodigy. "She was made for the camera," says her proud father. "She was natural, not plastic." At the age of eighteen months, Cindy made her debut in the first "bare-assed baby" Ivory Snow ad in 1959. When she was ten, she graduated to soap operas. By this time the child actress had appeared in one hundred and fifty commercials. Of her famous Polaroid ad, Cindy best remembers "the neat old man who drove the hansom cab," whom she has since tried, without success, to locate. She also remembers recording a song that was to play in the ad: "I love the zoo/ The kangaroo and the monkeys that swing in the air/But I love the zoo mostly because my daddy takes me there . . ." And Cindy recalls her disappointment when DDB decided to use Leigh's music instead. "I also thought it was funny that my Dad wore glasses, because he never wore them in real life." Her father was then seen weekly on *That Was the Week That*

Was, and the commercial-makers felt he might be recognized from the popular satirical program, so they disguised him with glasses. Cindy, "a ham since day one," appeared in a number of commercials because "I had a reputation in those days as a kid who wouldn't cry or throw a tantrum or ruin a day's work, so I was hired a lot." Her Polaroid ad was her favorite. "Every time it came on TV, someone would scream and we'd tear down the hallway to take a look."

"I grew up in New York and I went to public schools—ghetto schools, really—because my parents thought it would be good for a little prima donna like me. Here I was, making all this money and then playing with kids who couldn't afford a winter coat."

She grew familiar with the New York production company soundstages, clambering up a mountain of peanuts for a Crackerjack ad, or eating bar after bar of ice cream. "I grew up fast. I learned all the dirty jokes before anyone else. But even when I was small I felt privileged, and I felt I was learning a very special skill."

The noted Polaroid commercials after "Zoo" included a similarly memorable ad entitled "Train," which told the story of a family reunion at a railway station, preserved in Polaroid snapshots. Laurence Olivier appeared in

A father inspects his Polaroid pictures in a hansom cab, reliving his excursion with his daughter to the zoo. (Doyle Dane Bernbach, 1963)

Mariette Hartley eyes James Garner wryly as he explains Polaroid's One Step camera. Viewers were convinced that Hartley and Garner, who were so natural and informal, had to be man and wife. They were, in fact, a well-matched pair whose chemistry mixed in more than three hundred commercials. (Doyle Dane Bernbach, 1977)

the early seventies as an elegant pitchman—"the *Polaroid*" he would enunciate with his rolling Shakespearean vowels. But it was the James Garner–Mariette Hartley vignettes that would become the company's most memorable classics. Begun in 1977 to introduce the new One Step camera, the ads not only sent sales "through the roof," but convinced the nation that Garner and Hartley, who traded ironic quips while doing their pitches and who enjoyed a relaxed, informal relationship on camera, were in fact man and wife. In truth, Garner was initially signed to do the ads solo. The script for the third ad of the series which would eventually number more than three hundred commercials, called for a woman to appear. Bob Gage, the Doyle Dane Bernbach art director who directed and edited the scripts, which he wrote with Jack Dillon, remembered Hartley from a Pillsbury commercial, and cast her. The chemistry between James Garner, whom Gage calls "one of the most-liked guys in the United States," and Mariette Hartley created such a sensation that Hartley began appearing on TV talk shows wearing a T-shirt inscribed with the message, "I AM *NOT* MRS. JAMES GARNER." Nevertheless, Hartley, who had been an actress on TV and in movies for several years, freely acknowledges that the Polaroid ads, in which she prods Garner with wry looks and acerbic comments and then charms him with a smile, made her a household name.

During the seventies, when the standard sixty-second commercial had been largely replaced by the thirty-second ad due to the escalating cost of television time (a continuing inflation; ABC-TV's price tag to air a minute-long ad during the 1984 Olympic Games will approach half a million dollars), one sponsor, the Hallmark Card Company, produced a series of sentimental ninety-second mini-dramas that, to this day, remain some of TV's most touching commercials. The sponsor enjoyed a luxury of time since it was obliged to fill all the commercial slots on its *Hallmark Hall of Fame* program. One early landmark effort, 1971's "What a Day!" (see page 54), was a naturalistic ad that was one of the first to depict a woman as a human being and not as an obsessive housewife or vacuous glamour girl. Hallmark's agency, Foote, Cone & Belding of Chi-

cago, which had employed Walt Topel, the superb commercial director, on "What a Day!" brought him back in 1976 to do "Freddie and Sam."

In this story about a lifelong friendship, told in flashback, Sam tells how one night, when he and Freddie were preschoolers, they sat beneath the front porch of his mother's Charterville home and took an oath. Freddie made Sam cross his heart and "promise we'll always be best friends our whole life. No matter what Jimmy Baker says." Sam promises, but is soon heartbroken when Freddie's family moves away. At Christmas he is surprised by a card that assures him, "You're still my best friend." This begins the tradition of exchanging Christmas cards until, years later, Freddie's card announces a visit to Charterville. "Well, I saw Freddie that Christmas," Sam narrates, "and had she ever changed!" Indeed, the excited woman who emerges from the train at the station is a raven-haired beauty whom Sam later marries, climaxing their lifelong friendship.

"The response we received from 'Freddie and Sam' was amazing," says Jim McDowell, national advertising manager for the Kansas City-based greeting-card company. "People wrote to use saying it was their favorite commercial. And we've run it every year since." Another 1976 Hallmark ad, titled "Moving Day," also drew a great deal of viewer response. In this gentle vignette, produced by EUE/Screen Gems in Hollywood, a grandmother is sifting through all the greeting cards she has collected over the years. She sits in a pool of dusty light up in the attic while movers prepare to take her from her Victorian home. Like Ma Jode in *The Grapes of Wrath*, the woman is overcome with emotion as she examines the mementoes of a lifetime. Her grandson asks about the decades of old greeting cards, and she relates some of their stories. A granddaughter rummaging through a trunk nearby discovers an elaborate Easter bonnet, which she places on the woman's head before she and her brother run downstairs. Alone, the woman spies herself in a looking glass and smiles with the satisfaction of knowing she has lived a full life, and that her memories, as the announcer tells us, are "safe and secure" in the tangible form of greeting cards.

FCB

DATE: November, 1976
PRODUCER: Topel and Associates/Chgo.

CLIENT: Hallmark Cards, Inc.
PRODUCT: Christmas Custom
FILM NO.: HA76T14
FILM TITLE: "Freddie and Sam"

FILM LENGTH: :120
(Page 1 of 2)

1. (Music under throughout) NARRATOR: I remember when it all became official between Freddie and me.

2. We were home in Charterville... under mom's front porch.

3. FREDDIE: Promise we'll always be best friends our whole life...

4. SAM: Promise...

5. FREDDIE: No matter what Jimmy Baker says?...

6. SAM: Cross my heart. NARRATOR: Well, Freddie moved away right after that...

7. ...ah--and I remember how lonely I was...'til Christmas came, that is...

8. MOM: Sam...Sam,...

9. ...here's a Christmas card from Freddie's parents.

10. SAM: (Rather sad) Ohhhh,...

11. MOM: And there's a message in it for you, from Freddie...

12. SAM: There is!

13. MOM: There sure is, look!

14. FREDDIE'S VOICE OVER: (As Sam reads it) Dear Sam, My Dad and me built a double decker tree house...

15. ...and I got a hamster named Gerald... (CONTINUED)

A Southern California surfer shows that he is part of the sixties' "Pepsi Generation." Not only did the sponsor appropriate an entire age group, but it claimed a young generation that all the other generations hoped to emulate in appearance and outlook. (BBD&O, 1963)

These Hallmark commercials can still be seen during the breaks of the *Hall of Fame* presentations. And as they continue to air, year after year, these mini-dramas have become mementoes in their own right, video equivalents of seasonal greeting cards.

The season for Pepsi-Cola, and its often sentimental commercials, seems to be the endless summer. The soda pop's fast-paced "Pepsi Generation" ads did their bit to add to the sensory overload of the turbulent sixties. An anthemlike jingle, "You've got a lot to live, and Pepsi's got a lot to give," played while scores of tan, thin young people surfed and water-skied and fueled their beach parties with gallons of Pepsi-Cola in commercials that seemed scarcely able to contain all the activities crammed into them. The technique was continued in the seventies with the "Join the Pepsi People, Feelin'

Free" campaign. Just as the consumer of the fifties wanted to "Be Sociable, Be Smart" by drinking Pepsi, and as those of the sixties desired to be among "those who think young," so did the seventies' viewers want to "feel free" to pursue the good life. In 1975, this campaign engendered an ad called "Puppies," which, according to Alan Pottasch of the Purchase, New York-based Pepsi-Cola Company, "became our all-time classic, the most popular and most successful commercial in Pepsi history."

Halfway through the story, which follows a young family on its vacation at Grandma's rural home, a small, blond-haired boy begins to romp with a litter of puppies. Up to this point the images quickly followed one another and the chorus has sung fortissimo in the best Pepsi commercial tradition. Suddenly all is silent, and the viewer is treated to an extended, can-

"Have a Pepsi Day!" was the cola's greeting of the early seventies. Quick editing and tuneful jingles were the trademarks of Pepsi's commercials, which were filled with young people having fun. (BBD&O, 1973)

A little boy is overwhelmed by both his puppies and the giggles in one of commercials' most riotous moments. (BBD&O, 1975)

did view of the boy and his bouncing pets. The puppies knock him down and nearly overrun him as he thrashes about, helpless with laughter.

This was, simply, one of television's most singular and affecting moments, and it was wholly spontaneous. "To get something that natural and unrehearsed," says Pottasch, "you have to keep the cameras rolling and rolling. And whenever possible, we use real people instead of professional actors. Naturalism is important in our commercials. They capture people in the act of being themselves." The boy in "Puppies" is named Chad Bartholomew and those are really his dogs.

"Papa," the ad that formed the centerpiece for the 1980 campaign "Catch That Pepsi Spirit!" contained several "human" moments.

"Papa," an elderly but spirited European immigrant, arrives in New York at the opening of the ad. Veteran actor Harry Davis, who played Papa, says he "felt my father in me" as he walked off the same type of cargo steamer that had brought his parents to the New World at the turn of the century. "It was all there. The docks, the atmosphere, even the people seemed like those who would have welcomed my father."

In the ad, Papa is embraced by his son, whom he has not seen in years, and is whisked off to Brooklyn Heights. There the emotional reunion continues with an effusive block party. Beneath a banner strung across the street, proclaiming "WELCOME TO THE U.S.A.," Papa plays with the children and then spots an old flame whom he last saw in the Old Country.

"Papa" is hoisted by his family and neighbors in the New World, who toast him with Pepsi. (BBD&O, 1980)

Hamming it up, he and the woman enthrall the crowed with a native folk dance. We leave Papa, who had looked so doubtful when his ship docked, in the warm embrace of family, friends, and a new land. There is no dialogue in the ad, only music. But the fullness of its atmosphere and characterizations made this yet another classic "movie in a minute."

Coca-Cola, one of television's most prolific advertisers, and Coke's agency, McCann-Erickson, were responsible for the immensely popular 1979 commercial, "Mean Joe Greene." The Mean Joe in question was the bearded, 260-pound linebacker who earned his bone-crunching reputation when he demolished the opponents of the Pittsburgh Steelers. Greene has been injured in the opening of the Coke commercial and is surlier than ever as he limps past stadium spectators and down a tunnel toward the locker room.

A nervous boy watches his idol, Pittsburgh Steeler Mean Joe Greene, limp down a stadium tunnel. (McCann-Erickson, 1979)

A small boy holding a large bottle of Coca-Cola speaks to him nervously: "Mr. Greene? Need any help?"

"No, no thanks," snarls the football giant, colossal in his shoulder pads but wincing from the pain in his leg.

"Mr. Greene, I just want you to know"— the boy struggles as Greene stares at him impatiently—"I just want you to know that— that you're the greatest!"

Greene snorts, "Yeah, sure." The boy, fetch-ingly played by Tommy Okun, dares to stop the lineman again. "Would you like my Coke?"

"No, no thanks," Joe answers.

"It's okay. You can have it," the boy bravely persists, holding up the bottle. Joe relents. "Okay, thanks." He drains the bottle in a single gulp. Dejected, the boy turns and walks away, feeling he has failed to impress his idol. "See you around, Mean Joe."

Then Greene shouts to him, "Hey, kid! Catch." He tosses his jersey to the boy, who catches it in both arms, stammering with as-tonishment, "Thanks, Mean Joe!" Greene breaks into a broad smile, his "mean" reputa-tion now irreparably demolished.

Assisted by Penny Hawkey's dialogue and Lee Lacey's direction, Greene gave a first-rate

Mean Joe accepts the boy's Coke, which he proceeds to chugalug in one gulp. (McCann-Erickson, 1979)

performance that was continued in the 1982 made-for-TV move, *The Steeler and the Pitts-burgh Kid.* The film's story picks up Joe's rela-tionship with his young fan. While the NBC movie held the distinction of being the first fea-ture film to be based on a commercial, critics and viewers felt it was less emotionally satisfy-ing than its progenitor. But then, Coke's ad was a gem of a commercial, a perfect sixty seconds.

Conclusion

Up and Coming

Television is an entertainment medium. Even news programs recognize this fundamental reality. Certainly the TV commercial has to beguile in order to fulfill its function of establishing a product in the overtaxed consciousness of the consumer. Sex, humor, nostalgia, music, sentiment, and special effects have all been used by the thousands of talents who have created the commercials featured in this book, which represent only a fraction of the total number of video ads that have been produced since the dawn of the television age, thirty-five years ago. When one considers that it is the consumer who ultimately pays for the production of commercials, whose costs are included in the price of goods, it is a wonder that some grassroots revolt has not emerged to protest bad commercials and hold the classics up as examples of what might be done—what *should* be done.

The commercial has changed little since 1948. Its standard length has been shortened from one minute to thirty seconds as the cost of television time has escalated. The conclusion of the Golden Age of television commercials, which began during the mid-sixties and ended with the Nixon recession of 1970, coincided with the acceptance of the thirty-second ad. The possibilities for humor and storytelling were cut neatly in half. Television time continues to grow more expensive, and talk of even shorter commercials, three per sixty-second slot, is heard. These, if produced, would prove little more than video billboards. Other than length, little change is to be expected, although, with no governmental restrictions keeping them off the air, ads for handguns and hard liquor offer grotesque new possibilities for commercial-makers. Video ads for "Saturday-night specials" will doubtless never become reality, though, since television stations loathe controversy even more than they cherish advertising revenues.

Taken together, commercials provide a unique perspective on the consumer society that is the root of American culture. Certainly, video ads have influenced that culture. And, as significantly, they represent a new pop art discipline as intricate as Japanese haiku, for thirty seconds is all the time that commercial-makers have to tell their stories. The skill needed to synthesize music, plot, dance, animation, and other elements into these half-minutes is unique. By stingily making the most of every second as time itself increasingly becomes the most precious commodity, advertisers have unwittingly expanded the capabilities of television and film as they strive to make an impression. *Ars gratia artis* has never been the philosophy of commercial sponsors; it has been *Ars gratia pecuniae*—art for the sake of money. But a pop art form is the inadvertent result, all the same.

Index